PIF

WRITERS SERIES 34
SERIES EDITORS
JOSEPH PIVATO & ANTONIO D'ALFONSO

PIER GIORGIO DI CICCO

ESSAYS ON HIS WORKS

EDITED BY JOSEPH PIVATO

GUERNICA

TORONTO — BUFFALO — LANCASTER (U.K.)

2011

Joseph Pivato, Guest editor
Guernica Editions Inc.
P.O. Box 117, Station P, Toronto (ON), Canada M5S 2S6
2250 Military Road, Tonawanda, N.Y. 14150-6000 U.S.A.

Distributors:
University of Toronto Press Distribution,
5201 Dufferin Street, Toronto (ON), Canada M3H 5T8
Gazelle Book Services, White Cross Mills, High Town,
Lancaster LA1 4XS U.K.

First edition.
Printed in Canada.

Legal Deposit –Second Quarter
Library of Congress Catalog Card Number: 2011921285
Library and Archives Canada Cataloguing in Publication
Pier Giorgio Di Cicco : essays on his works / edited by Joseph Pivato.
(Writers series ; 34)
Includes bibliographical references.
ISBN 978-1-55071-313-8

1. Di Cicco, Pier Giorgio, 1949- --Criticism and interpretation.
I. Pivato, Joseph II. Series: Writers series (Toronto, Ont.) ; 34
PS8557.I248Z85 2011   C811'.54   C2010-906770-3

Contents

Introduction

JOSEPH PIVATO

Part One

Pier Giorgio Di Cicco has published over twenty books of poetry and has an impressive literary legacy. He is an author who is trans-national since he deals with his Italian cultural roots, his American childhood and his adult years as part of the Canadian literary scene. Italian words often appear in his writing. His poems often speak for and to a lost generation of immigrant children who grew up in Canada confused about their identity. His poems are much anthologized, quotable and leave a lasting impression. Nevertheless, at the height of his literary career, he changed direction.

After publishing fourteen books, Di Cicco entered a monastery in 1983 and stopped publishing for fifteen years. His last book was *Virgin Science* in 1986. When he returned to publishing in 2001, he was Father Pier Giorgio Di Cicco, a Roman Catholic priest who had been serving the Italian communities in the Toronto area for years. He was another Pier Giorgio Di Cicco but in some ways similar to the poet from the 1970s. In this collection we have included essays and an interview by writers who only met this Father Giorgio and speak about the spiritual dimensions of his writing and his life. They bring fresh perspectives to his work which are not influenced by the image of the Bloor Street poet with the black leather jacket who spent late nights drinking espresso, smoking and arguing about the role of the writer. For an impression of the Bloor Street poet see the essay by Mary di Michele, "Living Inside the Poem."

In addition to his own substantial body of work, Di Cicco has contributed in two other ways to Canadian literature: the initiation of Italian-Canadian writing and the establishment of the Association of Italian-Canadian Writers.

As recognition for his contributions to Canadian culture, Di Cicco was appointed Poet Laureate of Toronto for 2004-2007. During his tenure as Poet Laureate, Di Cicco worked on fostering a more creative city from human-scale architecture to openness to all the arts. He published his talks in *Municipal Mind: Manifestoes for the Creative City* (2007). Di Cicco's concerns with city living as expressed in his poems are explored in Domenic Beneventi's essay "The Urban Poetry of Pier Giorgio Di Cicco," and in

Jim Zucchero's essay "Di Cicco in the 21st Century." In his essay, "To Speak For, To Write To," Joshua Lovelace examines Di Cicco's strong sense of community.

Part Two

Pier Giorgio Di Cicco began Italian-Canadian writing and changed Canadian literature. On November 12, 1976, I received a letter from *Books in Canada* which read in part:

> I am preparing an anthology of Italo-Canadian poets … I'd be very pleased to consider a selection of your poetry for inclusion in the anthology. I would prefer poetry that is obviously Italianate in subject or theme or concern, though I am by no means restricted to that.

The letter was signed: Pier Giorgio Di Cicco, Assistant Editor. I responded with a two-page letter inquiring about the nature of the anthology, supporting the idea of publishing the work of Italian-Canadian artists, sharing my ideas about the Italian experience and promising to send some poems for him to consider.

In his return letter of November 16, Di Cicco explained that the anthology was to be in English, and he wrote:

> I want poems that speak about the Italian poet in Canada ... I assure you you are not alone in sharing; one of the purposes, in fact the prime purpose of this anthology is to band together poets like ourselves, of similar concerns.

With that idea for an anthology, Di Cicco had begun the development of Italian-Canadian literature which has now grown to include over 100 published writers working in English, in Italian and in French. This is a significant legacy to leave any community, in addition to his own works.

This collection of essays on Di Cicco is designed to examine his achievements as a poet and editor and his support for other writers.

The poems which Di Cicco collected and edited in 1976-77 became *Roman Candles: An Anthology of Seventeen Italo-Canadian Poets* which appeared in June, 1978. He spent that summer promoting the anthology by giving readings with other contributors from Ontario. In October of that year, he visited Edmonton where he gave readings at Athabasca University, the University of Alberta, and the Dante Society. He also gave a TV interview.

In the years that followed the appearance of *Roman Candles* several of the seventeen contributors went on to publish their own books of poems: Mary di Michele, *Tree of August* (1978) and *Mimosa and Other Poems* (1980); Filippo Salvatore, *Suns of Darkness* (1980); Mary Melfi, *A Queen is Holding a Mummified Cat* (1982); Alexandre Amprimoz, *Selected Poems* (1979); and Antonino Mazza, *The Way I Remember It* (1992). Len Gasparini, who had already published books of poems, brought out *Breaking and Entering* (1980).

In Toronto, Di Cicco taught creative writing and conducted poetry workshops where he encouraged other writers such as Gianna Patriarca, *Italian Women and Other Tragedies* (1994), and Dorè Michelut, *Loyalty to the Hunt* (1986). And there was the wider circle of writers which included Susan Glickman, Albert Moritz, Carolyn Smart, Roo Borson, Kim Maltman, Barry Dempster, Robert Priest, Dave Donnell and others. One member of this wide circle is Mary di Michele who contributes a contemplative essay here, "Living Inside the Poem."

Anthologies were an important way of establishing the credibility of Italian-Canadian writing. In Quebec the seminal anthology was *Quêtes: Textes d'auteurs italo-québécois* (1983) edited by Fulvio Caccia and Antonio D'Alfonso. In Toronto Caroline di Giovanni edited *Italian Canadian Voices* (1984), a project helped by Di Cicco and myself. Marisa De Franceschi edited

Pillars of Lace: The Anthology of Italian-Canadian Women Writers (1998). The most complete collection with fifty-three authors is *The Anthology of Italian-Canadian Writing* (1998) edited by myself.

It all started with *Roman Candles*. In the preface to that seminal anthology Di Cicco wrote:

> In 1974 I returned to Italy for the first time in twenty-odd years. I went, biased against a legacy that had made growing up in North America a difficult but not impossible chore (or so I thought). I went out of curiosity, and came back to Canada conscious of the fact that I'd been a man without a country for most of my life. And I became bitter at the thought that most people carry on day after day deeply aware that they do so on the land upon which they were born. It became clear to me that they had something immediately and emotionally at stake with their environment.
>
> And that phenomenon was something I had had to construct at every effort to feel relevant in an English country.
>
> So through the good grace of that foster agency, The Canada Council, I decided to do an anthology, banding together those poets whose work expressed this bicultural sensibility. I decided to limit the work to that written in English... but also to see what, if anything, these poets could bring to Anglo-Canadian poetry. In searching for contributions, I found isolated gestures by isolated poets, isolated mainly by the condition of nationalism prevalent in Canada in the last ten years (1970s). However plu-

ralistic the landscape seemed to be to sociologists, the sheer force of Canadianism had been enough to intimidate all but the older "unofficial-language" writers. Some of the contributors I had already been aware of through their publishing efforts, but most came as a surprise; and finally, all involved were surprised by the anthology itself. It put a stop to the aforementioned isolationism. (9)

Part Three

In September 1986, Di Cicco became one of the founding fathers of the Association of Italian-Canadian Writers. During a conference in Vancouver organized by Anna Foschi, Genni Gunn and the late Dino Minni, a number of the writers decided to establish an organization to unite writers of Italian background from across Canada. The other founding members were Antonio D'Alfonso, Mary di Michele, Pasquale Verdicchio, Marco Micone, Dorè Michelut, Antonino Mazza, Ken Norris, Francesco Loriggio, Franc Sturino, Roberta Sciff Zamaro, and myself.

Other writers joined the association later: Caterina Edwards, Fulvio Caccia, Frank Paci and Filippo Salvatore. The title of this first conference was "Italian-Canadian Writing in Transition: From Yesterday to Tomorrow," and it marked a turning point in these writers' self-awareness as they began to examine their publications, their preoccupations and their links to communities across Canada and in Italy. Di Cicco was one of the speakers who clearly articulated this self-reflection among the writers. The participants at that time were only half aware about Di Cicco's decision to join the religious life. The proceedings were later published as *Writers in Transition*, eds. C. Dino Minni and Anna Foschi Ciampolini (1990).

In some ways this Vancouver meeting was a continuation of the 1984 conference in Rome. Organized by Roberto Perin who was then Director at the Canadian Academic Centre in Italy, the conference focused on "Writing About the Italian Immigrant Experience in Canada." Di Cicco, along with several other writers, were at this meeting in Palazzo Cardelli in Rome, but it was dominated by historians and sociologists who were studying the different Italian immigrant communities in North America. The writers felt the need to have other meetings to deal with their own literary questions. So Dino Minni, who was not in Rome, invited everyone to Vancouver during Expo '86.

One of the goals in establishing the Association of Italian-Canadian Writers was to have regular meetings across Canada in order to promote local authors and support their publications. Di Cicco strongly supported these goals. The AICW has been able to achieve these objectives by having a national meeting every second year in a different city. In 1988 the second conference was held in Toronto and organized by myself, then holding The Mariano Elia Chair in Italian-Canadian Studies at York University.

In 1990 the third conference was in Ottawa and organized by Francesco Loriggio, professor at Carleton University. Di Cicco participated actively in all these meetings. At this Ottawa conference we also met three Italian-Australian writers.

The fourth meeting in 1992 was in Montreal and organized by Antonio D'Alfonso, director of Guernica Editions. The fifth was in 1994 in Winnipeg and organized by Caterina Sotiriadis. Number six was in Toronto in 1996 organized by myself from Edmonton. In 1998 we returned to Vancouver with Pasquale Verdicchio. In 2000 we returned to Montreal to a meeting organized by Licia Canton and Domenic Cusmano.

Canton edited the proceedings, *The Dynamics of Cultural Exchange* (2002). Ryerson University hosted the ninth meeting in Toronto in 2002 with Francesca L'Orfano as the organizer. In 2004 the University of Udine hosted an international meeting organized by Anna Pia De

Luca. The proceedings, *Shaping History* (2005), were edited by Anna Pia De Luca and Alessandra Ferraro. For the twentieth anniversary reunion in 2006 we returned to Vancouver to an event organized by Peter Oliva of Calgary. The proceedings were published as *Strange Peregrinations* (2007) eds. Delia De Santis, Venera Fazio & Anna Foschi Ciampolini. In 2008 the twelfth meeting was at the Frank Iacobucci Centre, University of Toronto. In 2010 the thirteenth meeting took place in Atri, Italy.

George Elliott Clarke has pointed to the publishing projects, the anthologies and the conferences of Italian-Canadian writers as models that other ethnic minority groups should follow in promoting their own cultures and literatures in the larger multicultural world of Canada. He has an essay here discussing Italian-Canadian and African-Canadian anthologies. We now accept that linguistic diversity is one of the markers of ethnic minority writing in Canada and is part of Canadian literature.

Part Four

Italian-Canadian writers helped the larger Italian community rediscover its history. The forgotten first Italian writer in Canada was Francesco

Giuseppe Bressani who published his *Breve Relatione* in Italian in 1653. We now have schools, streets, parks and a literary prize named after Bressani. This Jesuit missionary killed by the Iroquois is now a hero.

From its beginnings in ethnic newspapers in the 1920s, Italian-Canadian writing has existed in English, French and Italian. Liborio Lattoni wrote in Italian while Francesco M. Gualtieri published in English. *La Ville sans femmes* (1945) by Mario Duliani appeared in French and later in Italian as *Citta senza donne*. Gianni Grohovaz, Elena Randaccio and Guglielmo Vangelisti (*Gli Italiani in Canada*, 1956), who published in the 1950s in Italian, were followed by authors who actively participated in both the growth of Canadian literature and the flowering of multiculturalism, thus making an impact on mainstream English and French Canadian writing. This was the context and the fertile ground for a new literature to spring up and flourish.

Di Cicco had the insight to see possibilities for uniting writers of Italian background. The breakthrough came with *Roman Candles* (1978). However, the impact was not immediate. Writers in the different languages continued to publish unaware of one another. The trilingual tradition continued with Alexandre Amprimoz's *Fragments of Dreams* (1982), followed by *Sur le damier des tombes* (1983); Filippo Salvatore's *La Fresque de Mussolini* (1985); Romano Perticarini's *Quelli della fionda* (1981); Maria Ardizzi's *Made in Italy* (Italian and English editions,1982); and Antonio D'Alfonso's *The Other Shore* (1986). Gradually poets included in *Roman Candles* brought out their own books and demonstrated that the anthology was not an anomaly.

Diverse themes on language and identity began to appear in the books of younger poets: Pasquale Verdicchio's *Moving Landscape* (1985), Fulvio Caccia's *Irpenia* (1983), Lisa Carducci's *Cris et palpitations* (1989) and Genni Gunn's *Mating in Captivity* (1993).

At about the time that Di Cicco was collecting Italian-Canadian poems for his anthology, novelist Frank Paci was finishing his first book, *The Italians*, which appeared the same year as *Roman Candles*. Like the other fiction authors, Paci focused on chronicling the immigrant experience: *Black Madonna* (1982), *The Father* (1984), and *Under the Bridge* (1992). Other works of fiction in the realist tradition – Caterina Edwards' *The Lion's Mouth* (1982) and *Island of the Nightingales* (1994), and Marisa De Franceschi's *Surface Tension* (1994) – explore women's views on ethnic identity. When Nino Ricci won the Governor General's Literary

Award in fiction for *Lives of the Saints* (1990), many Italian-Canadian writers began to receive more attention. Anecdotal stories by Dino Minni (*Other Selves*, 1985), Darlene Madott (*Bottled Roses*, 1985, *Joy, Joy, Why Do I Sing*, 2004), Michael Mirolla (*The Formal Logic of Emotion*, 1991), Genni Gunn (*On the Road*, 1991), Delia De Santis (*Fast Forward*, 2008), and Licia Canton (*Almond Wine and Fertility*, 2008) highlight the ironies and joys of life on the margins of mainstream society. In Peter Oliva's *Drowning in Darkness* (1993), the narrators experiment with magic realism. There also appeared a number of plays by Edwards, Marco Micone, Melfi, Vittorio Rossi, Frank Canino and Tony Nardi.

In Quebec Italian writers are identified by their diversity: Tonino Caticchio writing in his Roman dialect; Dominique De Pasquale's French plays; Bianca Zagolin's French novels; Elettra Bedon's Italian stories; Lisa Carducci writing in French and Italian; Marco Fraticelli's English haiku poems; Corrado Mastropasqua's Neapolitan poems; and Camillo Menchini re-writing histories in Italian. The two most successful writers are Fulvio Caccia who won a Governor General's Award for French poetry with *Aknos* (1994) and who is also known for his short stories and essays; and Marco Micone who won awards for his plays, *Gens du silence* (1982) and *Addolorata* (1984). Carole David and Antonio D'Alfonso both experiment with French prose-poems and poetic narratives. This diversity is reflected in the founding of Guernica Editions as a trilingual press in Montreal in 1978 and its promotion of writers in all three languages.

Italian-Canadian literature received academic recognition with the anthologies, but also through the literary studies that appeared: *Contrasts* (1985) and *Echo* (1994) by Joe Pivato; *Devils in Paradise* (1997) by Pasquale Verdicchio; *Social Pluralism and Literary History* (1994), edited by Francesco Loriggio; and *Adjacencies* (2004), eds. Lianne Moyes, Licia Canton and Domenic Beneventi. Many other books and articles relating in whole or in part to the Italian-Canadian experience have also been published.

The literary criticism of these writers and academics also stimulated the work of writers from other backgrounds: Christl Verduyn, ed. *Literary Pluralities* (1998); Lien Chao, *Beyond Silence: Chinese Canadian Literature in English* (1997); Nurjehan Aziz, ed. *Floating the Borders: New Contexts in Canadian Criticism* (1999); George Elliott Clarke, *Odysseys Home: Mapping African-Canadian Literature* (2002); Eleanor Ty and Christl Verduyn, *Beyond Autoethnography: Asian Canadian Writing* (2008), among other examples.

This collection of essays on Di Cicco is a testament to his achievements as a writer, but also to the success of Italian-Canadian literature.

Works Cited

Di Cicco, Pier Giorgio, ed. *Roman Candles: An Anthology of Poems by Seventeen Italo-Canadian Poets*. Toronto: Hounslow Press, 1978.

Canadian Ethnic Ironies and Di Cicco's Poetry

LINDA HUTCHEON

I enter here upon the general area of ethnicity and race with much interest and not a little trepidation: interest, because of my own Italian-Canadian ethnic background (I was a Bortolotti before becoming a Hutcheon); trepidation, because of the manifest and multiple risks any such discussion entails. Some of these have been suggested in an article by Robert Harney that, in the context of its attack on Canadian multicultural ideals, has to have one of the most intentionally ironic titles around: "So Great a Heritage as Ours: Immigration and the Survival of the Canadian Polity." In this article, Harney makes a distinction in terminology between "immigrant" and "ethnic": "to be called ethnic in Canada is to be called less, as in 'ethnic writer,' and marginal as in 'ethnic enclave'" (68). This explains in his mind, the attraction of the word "multicultural" (79). Certainly, if the term "ethnic" were limited, as it usually is, to non-Anglo or non-French, then the associations have indeed traditionally been of "less" and "marginal" within what was once called the "vertical mosaic" of Canadian social hierarchies. Enoch Padolsky's answer to Harney and other critics has been to argue that we use the term "ethnic minority" to indicate our understanding that the English and the French majorities in Canada are also ethnic groups who possess distinctive cultural customs and languages (113). So an Italian-Canadian writer such as Pier Giorgio Di Cicco could be called an ethnic minority author.

Theorists of ethnicity have also made the distinction between ethnicity as a lived experience of "otherness," and ethnicity as governed, packaged, marketed, and consumed – in Canada, as multiculturalism. While not denying that difference, nor denigrating that experience of alienation (which I know my own family has faced), I still find myself reacting against the seemingly cynical view of Canadian multiculturalism that this suggests. And yet there is a distinction to be made between multiculturalism as lived and multiculturalism as the rewriting of ethnic history as well as present life from the point of view of the dominant Anglo/French cultures. Multiculturalism maps differences – and legitimizes them through government support for things like academic, literary and historical research and also the various ethnic festivals and events held across the nation. But mapping difference can be a positive as well as a negative thing; it can be a way both of celebrating those differences (while still remaining within Canadian culture) and resisting assimilation. And I think that irony is one of the discursive strategies used by such marginalized or minority artists to signal that resistance – perhaps even that celebration. We certainly find this kind of "ethnic" irony in *Roman Candles*, the seminal anthology edited by Di Cicco. In one of the poems included in this Italian-Canadian collection, "Canadese," Antonino Mazza uses irony with a certain deconstructive, critical power:

> Because life for him
> has been labour and struggle,
> Canadese, remember your father.
> Don't try to reject your mother tongue,
> in our cage, it is wrong;
> do canaries smother their private song?
> Be patient, don't rage,
> Canadese, in time we'll belong;
> we'll acquire our own sense of the land;
> we'll record life and death of our million births;
> we'll have families
> above and below the earth.
> Canadese, you must never forget
> what you are... never
> because, when you do, they'll remind you. (39)

The addressee of this poem – the "you" – is

specifically an Italian-Canadian, ironically called "Canadese," the Italian term for Canadian, and so my response here is likely different from that of most readers. The ethnicity of the implied reader is an issue not often addressed in studies of ethnic writing, yet the "we/they" doubleness, which the irony of this poem foregrounds, is as much the basis of the politics of resistance as the source of the alienation of otherness. And doubleness – of identity, of culture, of loyalties, often of language – is the basis of the experience of immigration in general, for anyone, anywhere. But in Canada it continues to define the experience of those of any "different" ethnicity and race – different from the English and French white majorities.

In an important early essay on the "ethnic voice" in Canadian writing, Eli Mandel noted that doubleness, even "duplicity," was what all immigrants live and grapple with daily (265). The literature that comes out of this experience itself exists at "the interface of two cultures": "a form concerned to define itself, its voice, in the dialectic of self and other and the duplicities of self-creation, transformation, and identities" (274). I have been suggesting that irony is one way of coming to terms with this kind of duplicity, for it is the trope that incarnates doubleness, and it does so in ways that are particularly useful to the "other": irony allows "the other" to address the dominant culture from within that culture's own set of values and modes of understanding, without being co-opted by it and without sacrificing the right to dissent, contradict, and resist.

For immigrants the need to resist the dominant culture – however liberal or well-meaning – may be intensified because of the weight of cultural tradition, made heavier (not lighter) by distance and time, by memory, by a sense of exile or simple nostalgia. Therefore the drive towards self-definition within a new culture may well involve separation from this ethnic past, at least temporarily. And irony is a useful device for articulating both the pull of that tradition and the need to contest it. It is also a way to challenge ethnic stereotyping. In his ironic poem in *Roman Candles*, Len Gasparini writes to Di Cicco, as a fellow poet:

> Let us string our mandolins and sing
> O Sole Mio every night.
> The joy is ours.
> Strangled by a spaghetti stereotype,
> an Italian is supposed to lay bricks.
> You build poems with the stars. (27)

In *A Poetics of Postmodernism*, I argue that what we currently call postmodernism has entailed a re-valuing of difference in culture: difference in terms of gender, race, ethnicity, class, sexual preference. The "ex-centric" or off-centre is valued over the centre (57-73). The postmodern distrust of centres and the hierarchies they imply can be seen in many ways: in the recoding of the (denigrated) notion of regionalism into the positive concept of the local and specific; in the focusing of attention on the periphery rather than the metropolis; and in the general interest in diversity, in the different rather than the same. Part of this is simply an inversion of pre-existing hierarchies, since all binaries indeed conceal hierarchies, as Jacques Derrida has taught us. Poststructuralist thought like his has also suggested that all meaning is created by differences and is sustained by reference to other meaning. So, while this equally binary inversion operates as a powerful challenge to the established power of centres (of economic, political, social, and cultural power), the postmodern also tries to go beyond this and to rethink binary oppositions completely in terms of the multiple, the plural, and the heterogeneous: "and/also" thinking replaces "either/or" thinking.

For literary and cultural studies, the end result of this postmodern reassessment has been a new cultivation of cultural difference as positively valued diversity and plurality. A good example of this kind of rethinking in the area of ethnicity is Werner Sollors' book, *Beyond Ethnicity: Consent and Descent in American Culture* (1986), which convincingly argues that ethnicity, despite predictions of its demise within industrialized urban North America, has flourished to the point that ethnic identity is considered a "sacred asset" rather than a "heathenish liability." While the experience of many North Americans might still belie such academic confidence, there is no doubt that ethnic and racial minorities play a very visible role in postmodern culture today. George Lipsitz has suggested that their "exclusion from political power and cultural recognition has enabled them to cultivate a sophisticated capacity for ambiguity, juxtaposition, and irony – all key qualities in the postmodern aesthetic" (159). One of the reasons for irony's key position in postmodernism, however, is that ex-centricity is what in fact defines the postmodern, and resistance to a dominant (from within) is part of that definition. Lipsitz points out that, since ethnic and racial minorities can neither assimilate nor separate completely from the dominant culture, they are forced into "complex and creative cultural negotiations" with and against the dominant force, negotiations that involve confronting it with their own history and traditions. Lipsitz even goes so far as to make the doubleness or "bifocality" of the

28

ethnic vision the paradigm for "the decentered and the fragmented nature of contemporary experience". In other words, ethnic (and presumably racial) minorities are paradoxically both marginal and typical: "Masters of irony in an ironic world, they often understand that their marginality makes them more appropriate spokespersons for society than mainstream groups unable to fathom or address the causes of alienation." Perhaps. But this kind of logic denies the specific kind of doubleness of the ethnic vision; it risks ignoring the *double* alienation that particular vision may represent in an already alienated and alienating world.

The politics of ethnicity and race are far too complex for me to address here. Instead I want to look at the politics of representation of ethnicity in some poems by Di Cicco in the context of Italian-Canadian writing. The range of modes of representation possible here is wide: from nostalgia or realistic portrayal to ironic signalling of the constructed nature of the representation. In the work of Robert Kroetsch, for example, there is a self-conscious awareness of the ideological as well as the aesthetic problems involved in representing "otherness." While many others have studied the themes and images of the immigrant, and even of race and ethnicity, in Canadian writing, my particular focus will be

limited to what irony reveals about the doubleness that everyone argues to be part of the experience of ethnicity. It is probably true that irony
is at least potential in not only anything doubled
but also anything problematic or relative. John
Roberts has shown how John Marlyn's novel
Under the Ribs of Death uses irony to evoke and
illuminate a world of shifting perspective that
leaves the immigrant protagonist confused and
alienated. This is one kind of situational irony
set up by the structural ironies in the plot.

Sometimes, however, the ironies are verbal,
as in so much of the work of those Winnipeg
writers educated in secular Yiddish schools:
Adele Wiseman, Jack Ludwig, Miriam Waddington, Larry Zolf, and others. While writing in
English, they have been able to draw on the
Jewish tradition's wealth of verbal wit and
humour that is often driven by irony. The same
is true of the writing of A.M. Klein and Leonard
Cohen, not to mention Mordecai Richler and
Irving Layton. Verbal ironies can also be seen in
the work of Mennonite writers, for whom language takes on a special significance as the willed
inscription of both community and difference.
For those who choose to write in English, and
not Low German or *plattdeutsch*, there is a constant tension between tongues that can often
take the form of irony. It can be broad, as in the

literalized dialectical play of Armin Wiebe's *The Salvation of Yasch Siemes*; or it can be more subtle and symbolic, as in Rudy Wiebe's *My Lovely Enemy*. For some Mennonite writers, that strong cultural tradition and its language are as much something to work against as to work with: Di Brandt's *questions i asked my mother* is one example of this, and not accidentally, it is by a woman.

A clear split between ironic and elegiac representations of ethnic experience is evident in Italian-Canadian writing, perhaps partly because the vast majority of this group emigrated more recently than some of the groups mentioned above. It is not surprising, I suppose, that what Joseph Pivato has called the "literature of exile" – be it written in the old language or the new – might focus less on the situational ironies of two cultures and more on the nostalgic yearning for the one left behind. The mode of writing here is often elegiac – the mode of loss and mourning. There is frequently less anger than affection, less resistance than testimonial. As poet Filippo Salvatore puts it:

> The generations of silence who worked hard to adapt to life in Canada, for financial success and the education of their children, watch with emotion as their exile, their sacrifice, their heroic determination and their need to forge new roots are finally being expressed. Whether the writing is in English, French,

31

or Italian, these writers of Italian origin feel the need to speak of their mothers and fathers in their works. This is our generation's confession of love and affection to our parents, and a way of remaining faithful to our roots. (201)

There would seem to be little room for irony here. The work of someone like Di Cicco – who can muster irony on so many occasions – provides a good example. There is bitterness, nostalgia, and sadness in the elegiac poem "Remembering Baltimore, Arezzo" (*Tough* 10) and "Man Without a Country" (*Burning* 25), but no real irony. And no real distance – which is perhaps the point. Where irony does come into Di Cicco's work is in some of the early self-reflexive and often satirical poems about poets and poetry in *A Burning Patience* with "Bar-Room Poets," "L'Artiste" and "The Outsiders". Di Cicco is ironic in some of the angry poems from his 1985 collection *Post-Sixties Nocturne* about urban consumer culture: "On the Up and Up," "Buying In" and "Ray R." Many of the poems here are reminiscent of his earlier, masterly ironic tours de force "Relationships" and "Male Rage Poem" (*Flying* 24 & 55), In the latter, the ironies begin in the title and gain in intensity as the poem progresses. "Male Rage Poem" opens with:

Feminism, baby feminism.
This is the anti-feminist poem
It will get called anti-
feminist poem. Like it or not.

The poet then lists why it will be so named,
ending the list with:

This is where the poem peters out... oops! – that's
penis mentality, that's patriarchal bullshit,
sexist diction and these line lengths are
male oriented.

The poem then goes on to attack the simplifica-
tions and reductions of feminist views of phallo-
centric culture, for this is what he sees as the real
cause of his "male rage". It comes:

From standing out like a man for a bunch of
years, and being called the dirty word.
"When you are 21 you will become a Man."
Christ! Doomed to enslave women ipso
facto, without even the right training for it.
Shouldn't have wasted ten years playing
baseball; should have practised
whipping...

The angry ironies continue to multiply:

I'm tired of being a man,
of having better opportunities,
better job offers,
too much money.

And these ironies are multi-directional; the targets, plural:

> Doc – give it to me straight.
> How long do I have before this male rage
> takes over completely?
> The rest of your life.
> Take it like a man!

The ironies here are gender-related, not particularly ethnic. Are certain things – like one's ethnicity – somehow taboo for irony? Or is it a matter of a group's needing distance and time? In *The Tough Romance*, Di Cicco has poems which come close to ironic distance: "The Elder," "America" and "Growing Up in Baltimore." Di Cicco sometimes uses the Italian language to create verbal irony. There are poems with Italian titles which suggest a sentiment or idea which is the opposite of what is expressed in the text. The poem "Canzone" has a title which evokes a romantic love song and the poem begins with images of beautiful tulips, but ends in anger and despair. And poems with titles, "Credo," "Gioventu" and "Ecco" suggest a number of things in Italian that are disconnected from the poems themselves. It is as if these titles become ethnic jokes.

What tends to happen when Italian-Canadian

writers express their feelings about their particular ethnic doubleness is that the dualities are translated more often into ambivalence and paradox than irony. For example, there is the "your/our" ambivalence in Salvatore's "My People":

I hate your meanness, admire
your courage, adore your tenacity.
[...]
It's our little joys, sufferings,
weaknesses, qualities, I hate and love
so much, people, my people
people as dear to me
as the early morning sun.

The potential for irony exists in the doubling pronominal oppositions, but it is not realized here. I do not mean to suggest, however, that it is totally absent from Italian-Canadian writing. My earlier citations of Gasparini and Mazza offer a few examples of where it can and does occur. Often, though, the ironies are less verbal than structural: such as the larger narrative ironies surrounding the character Marie in Frank Paci's novel *Black Madonna*. Doing all she can to flee her dominating Italian mother's control and influence, Marie chooses a profession, life-style, and spouse that are utterly the opposite of what would be expected for her as a young Italian-Canadian working-class woman from Northern Ontario. Yet, in the end, Marie is forced to see that all this flight has ironically led her only closer to that which she sought to escape. She repeats, in her relationship with her own child, the power games she used to resent her mother playing with her – especially over the issues of food. And her own anorexia – her way of controlling something in the face of her mother's food (the symbol of her domination) – ends up causing her to look just like that thin woman who was her mother.

Perhaps, then, one level at which to look for ironies in the representation of ethnicity is this level of structure, or what Robert Kroetsch has called the "grammar of the narrative of ethnic experience." Kroetsch's own examination of one such "grammar" reveals pairs of opposites: success/failure, inferiority/superiority, revelation/concealment, integration/resistance, erasure/memory (65). These are indeed the kind of binaries that engender the ironies of the unsaid/said at the level of structure.

Mary di Michele, one of the two women poets included in *Roman Candles*, captures ethnic irony with her poem, "Casa Mia," which anticipates the psychological ironies of her later work, *Mimosa* (1981). From its visual presentation on, *Mimosa* is a poem about doubleness and fragmentation, about the ideal and the real, the past and the present. The cover presents a photograph of the poet's "blond child" whom her father "loved too well," a photo that gets broken up like puzzle pieces or fragments of a shattered mirror image in its subsequent appearances in the book. The ironies inherent in the visual fragmentation are worked out in the formal juxtapositions of the three parts of the poem. The first section consists of the story of the disappointment and limited joys of nostalgia for an aging immigrant. Significantly, this is told from the point of view of Vito, the father, but in the third person: this is the silent generation, who must be spoken for by others and who can never entirely be known:

> There is only one heaven, the heaven of the home.
> There is only one paradise, the garden
> that kept them little children even as adults,
> until one angel, Lucia, his luckless offspring
> fell refusing to share in his light. (1)

The second part is the monologue of one of his daughters, Marta: this is the generation that has its own voice. But now the structural ironies begin. Vito had always thought Marta looked too much "like her mother" and had preferred the blonde daughter, Lucia. This parental preference sets up both the emotional dynamics and the structural ironies of the poem. Marta's monologue provides the reader with her perceptions of Vito's world and her own. Embedded in the ironies created by this difference of perspective is another level of ironic discrepancy: between what Marta does – and intends – and what she really feels. This level is underlined by her self-undermining self-awareness. This woman tells us that she works, lives at home, and offers "the proper respect to our relatives", but then undercuts all this in the next line: "I listen very carefully to all their bullshit." Marta berates her sister, Lucia, for not pretending, as she does, to like "uncle Joe/ whom she calls a macho pig", and counsels hypocrisy as a "safe" alternative to being outside the family altogether, a "gypsy" poet like Lucia. Her overt announcement of hypocrisy conditions any interpretation of all that she claims she does "as an act of love" for her family, as do her jealousy of Lucia and her desire for the love her father always gave to her sister. The third part of the poem, "Lucia's Monologue", offers further structural ironies in the juxtaposition with both of the preceding sections and points of view. It ends with her trying, in silence, to come closer to Vito, whom she resembles and loves. The final irony is that, although a poet, Lucia cannot express her love to him in words – except in this poem.

Di Michele can and does deploy verbal ironies in

her verse, but they are much more likely to appear in poems about male/female relationships or clichés of culture such as "How to Kill your Father", from *Bread and Chocolate*, and "Life is Theatre or to be Italian in Toronto drinking cappuccino on Bloor Street at Bersani & Carlevale", from *Stranger in You*. The pattern is similar to that found in the work of Di Cicco. Perhaps the experience of Italian immigrants has been more one of suffering, pain and death than joy – or even resistance. In Antonio D'Alfonso's poetic diary, *The Other Shore*, there is existential probing into art, love, family, even the ethnic past; there is self-reflexive, poetic self-analysis; there is languid meditation; but there is little irony. While the distance and separation that irony implies may be possible for many second-generation Italian-Canadian writers, relatively few choose to make use of their power when dealing with their ethnic roots, past or present. Why? For the second generation, perhaps the pains and pressures of immigration are less strong, leaving only an elegiac relation to the past. Generalizations, however, can only be rash. The complex structural and verbal ironies of Canadian-born Nino Ricci's portrayal of the fictional Italian village of Valle del Sole and its inhabitants in *Lives of the Saints* suggests that distance can allow something besides nostalgia.

In *The Anthology of Italian-Canadian Writing* (1998) Joseph Pivato tries to identify examples of ethnic irony by collecting them in a section, "Ironies of Identity." However, Italians in Canada may well have less cause for the kind of anger that can unleash the true fury of oppositional irony in the responses of other ethnic and racial groups. Remember: Di Cicco's irony is *not* aimed at ethnicity!

Note

The pages in this essay are edited excerpts from a chapter in my book, *Spitting Images: Contemporary Canadian Ironies*. Toronto: Oxford U.P., 1991. (47-68)

Works Cited

Di Cicco, Pier Giorgio. *A Burning Patience*. Ottawa: Borealis Press, 1978.
_____. *Flying Deeper into the Century*. Toronto: McClelland & Stewart, 1982.
_____. *Post-Sixties Nocturne*. Fredericton: Fiddlehead Poetry Books, 1985.
_____. *The Tough Romance*. Toronto: McClelland & Stewart, 1979.
_____. Ed. *Roman Candles*. Toronto: Hounslow Press, 1978.
Di Michele, Mary. *Mimosa and Other Poems*. Oakville: Mosaic Press, 1981.
_____. *Bread and Chocolate*. Ottawa: Oberon, 1980.
_____. "Life is Theatre," *Stranger in You*. Toronto: Oxford U.P. 1995.
Gasparini, Len. "Il Sangue," *Roman Candles*. 27.
Harney, Robert F. "So Great a Heritage as Ours: Immigration and the Survival of the Canadian Polity," *Daedalus* 117, 4 (1988), 51-98.
Hutcheon, Linda. *A Poetics of Postmodernism*. New York: Routledge, 1988.
Kroetsch, Robert. "The Grammar of Silence: Narrative Patterns in Ethnic Writing," *Canadian Literature* 106 (1985).

Lipsitz, George. "Cruising Around the Bloc – Postmodernism and Popular Music in East Los Angeles," *Cultural Critique* 5 (1986/87).

Mandel, Eli. "The Ethnic Voice in Canadian Writing," in *Figures in a Ground*. Eds Diane Bessai & Davis Jackel. Saskatoon: Western Producer Prairie Books, 1978.

Mazza, Antonino. "Canadese," *Roman Candles*. 39.

Paci, F.G. *Black Madonna*. Ottawa: Oberon, 1982.

Padolsky, Enoch. "Cultural Diversity and Canadian Literature: A Pluralistic Approach to Majority and Minority Writing in Canada." *International Journal of Canadian Studies* 3 (Spring 1991) 111-128.

Pivato, Joseph. "A Literature of Exile: Italian Language Writing in Canada," *Contrasts: Comparative Essays on Italian-Canadian Writing*. Montreal: Guernica, 1985.

_____. Ed. *The Anthology of Italian-Canadian Writing*. Toronto: Guernica, 1998.

Ricci, Nino. *Lives of the Saints*. Dunvegan: Cormorant Press, 1990.

Roberts, John. "Irony in an Immigrant Novel: John Marlyn's *Under the Ribs of Death*," *Canadian Ethnic Studies* 14, 1 (1982), 41-8.

Salvatore, Filippo. "The Italian Writer in Quebec: Language, Culture and Politics," *Contrasts*. 201.

_____. "My People", *Roman Candles*.16.

Sollors, Werner. *Beyond Ethnicity: Consent and Descent in American Culture*. New York: Oxford U.P., 1986.

Poetry of a Lost Generation

> I play the tunes my father used to know, my father used to
> sing in the attic of his loneliest thought,
> thinking up a street in Italy, or of carrying a daughter
> into an autumn park; you knew these songs over and over
> the songs of sun... (Burning 26)

We came in crowded immigrant ships called Saturnia, Vulcania, and Conte Biancamano. We came from small towns and villages, spent decades learning the language and trying to adjust to North American cities. We often had one name at home and another at school. We were forgetting our past. There was something missing.

When I first read the poems of Pier Giorgio Di Cicco in 1977, I was shocked. Here was a writer who was speaking for us, a forgotten generation of Italian kids who had grown up in Canada and did not know who we were. We also did not know what we were. Were we Italians like our parents who happened to be living in Canada through the accident of immigration?

Or were we Canadians of Italian backgrounds? We did not fit either of these troublesome identities. We were just trying to survive in a new, ever-changing society; and to fit in somehow. The sharp images in Di Cicco's poetry brought back a little-known and almost forgotten history. Despite our initial reluctance to revisit our roots, Di Cicco's powerful poetic voice made us listen and see some things for the first time.

Our parents had suffered through depression, dictatorship and war in Italy. Some of our fathers had been soldiers and then prisoners of war. They had known many deaths in their families and villages. They had survived all this to endure post-war poverty in Italy. Emigration was the only choice for thousands of Italian families. Their relatives in Italy were sad to see them go, but they were relieved as well. The family farm was saved from being split up yet again. With thousands of men and women leaving Italy, there were less people competing for the few jobs that eventually became available. These young immigrants in the New World often sent back money to support aging parents or help a brother or cousin start a small business. But these exiles who benefitted Italy directly and indirectly were soon forgotten as the European economic miracle of the late 1960s began to transform the old continent into a "New

America." Not only were they forgotten, but relatives back in Italy who did not want to be reminded of the former poverty were almost ashamed of these immigrants who came back to visit their hometowns and villages. As the sons and daughters of these exiles, we had lost the little Italian language we knew, and only communicated with our parents in a regional dialect sprinkled with English words. So the generation that Di Cicco was writing about, although born in Italy and even schooled there in part, no longer belonged there in any way, not even as tourists.

In the 1950s Italian popular music had many songs about departure, nostalgia and remembering a lost past. Our immigrant parents, like those of Di Cicco, listened to songs with titles like: "Terra Straniera," "Vola colomba bianca vola," "Non ti scordar di me," "Binario," and "Canto dell'emigrante." These songs kept alive the visions of an Italy left behind, but it was an imaginary Italy, for the country was rapidly changing through the 1960s and 1970s. These immigrant songs are still more popular in Italian communities in Canada, the U.S. and Australia than they are in Italy. The quotation above which begins this essay is from a Di Cicco poem called appropriate enough, "Immigrant Music." (Pivato 77-91).

Did we really feel we belonged in Canada? Not when we were growing up in the 1950s.

We were often made to feel as if we were from another race, an inferior race that was not too bright but good for manual labour. We had strange non-Canadian sounding last names with long vowels at the end. And even when the English/Irish nuns translated our Christian first names into English, they often came out sounding strange. We usually had one name at home and another one at school. We also had to learn a new language which meant that we were at a disadvantage academically. Many teachers encouraged us to go into technical trades; to work with our hands like our immigrant parents. Most of us did not even dream of going to university in the 1960s even thought university enrolments were exploding all over the North American continent. So the very few of us who did manage to complete a university degree where shocked to find a poet writing about us. Suddenly there was somebody writing about our experiences. Suddenly we were not alone, isolated and voiceless.

Di Cicco proved this when he edited an historic anthology for this lost generation in 1978. He called it *Roman Candles* which proved to be a fortuitous name since it went on to spark a whole library of books by Italian-Canadian writers, authors working in English, in French and in Italian. Giorgio was one of the first to sense that there was a number of writers scattered across the country who were speaking for this generation of young people forgotten both by Italy and Canada. He went on to encourage many of these writers – Mary di Michele, Filippo Salvatore, Mary Melfi – and began organizing meetings in the Toronto area. Eventually these meetings led to conferences and the founding of the Association of Italian-Canadian Writers in Vancouver in 1986.

This brief introduction is by way of background information for the poetry of Di Cicco which interests me here, his early poetry. The poems from the 1970s most often document incidents from his experiences of dislocation which speak to me and to many other people of this lost generation. They are poems which were initially stimulated by Giorgio's first return trip to Italy in 1974. In the "Preface" to *Roman Candles*, he articulated this awakening of his Italian roots with these words, quoted in the Introduction but worth repeating:

I went, biased against a legacy that had made growing up in North America a difficult but not impossible chore (or so I thought). I went out of curiosity, and came back to Canada conscious of the fact that I'd been a man without a country for most of my life. And I became bitter at the thought that most people carry on day after day deeply aware that they do so on the land upon which they were born. It became clear to me that they had something immediately and emotionally at stake with their environment. And that phenomenon was something I had had to construct at every effort to feel relevant in an English country. (9)

Di Cicco's early poetry is a reiteration of these sentiments of loss and alienation. His lyrics are unashamedly autobiographical to an extent that was not acceptable to proponents of the New Criticism or European Formalism. In the section, "The Man Without a Country," Di Cicco's apostrophe to Italy is heart-felt:

Italia bella, I return to you.
there is no question of lateness
for I was taken from you and cannot
remember the parting. (*Burning,* 25)

He often recalls his dead father and his dead brother. The war time events of his family are often alluded to, as is its dislocation to Canada and the United States. Di Cicco's subject matter and themes emerge from the forgotten social history which I summarized above. It is as if he cannot help but write out of this experience and speak for his lost, voiceless generation. What is also striking about his early poems is that we hear the clear distinct voice and see a new perspective. The poems made us see who we were. Di Cicco's apostrophe to Italy continues:

> I am that much of you, hearsay.
> I have traced your features over
> my needs over a continent where
> I found you out by what I could not love;
> patched myself up with
> what I hardly knew of you, Italia. (*Burning* 25)

The overwhelming impulse to deal with this material from personal history is evident in Di Cicco's first chapbook of verse, *We Are the Light Turning* (1975). Here his poem, "The Statue of Guido Monaco, Arezzo," is dedicated to the memory of his father. The personal voice comes through in poems printed in *The Grad Post* and *Dreadnaught 52* in 1976. In an early collection, *The Circular Dark* (1977), Di Cicco has a section devoted to his Italian trip and to members of his family. It begins with the idyllic poem, "Italy, 1974," which recalls a Tuscany of lovers in warm evenings and old men in the sun. It is a lament for a lost world and begins with the poet's wish to be part of this landscape:

> – nella campagna – couched between two hills
> in the circular dark I lay in the summer cool (34)

For a brief moment there is the illusion that, "the kinship between the speaker and the earth is repeatedly marked, thus constructing a subject that can claim a certain territoriality ... in the figurative repossession of the mother." (Blodgett, 629) The ultimate sense of loss is overwhelming, however, and is suggested by the use of the past tense. The happy return trip to Italy reminds the speaker, and us, of all that was lost, of all that was changed, forever.

In poem after poem, old Italian men and women appear. Familiar scenes and places are haunted by the dead. These Italians have a sense of belonging "in their fields" where they are born, work and die. In contrast to this sense of peace is the next poem, "Impersonation," about the poet's father dying of heart failure in a strange hospital, in a strange city. The disease has changed and aged his father so much that the poet no longer recognizes him. It is an impersonation of his father, or perhaps it is the speaker distancing himself from a dying man in order to lessen the sense of loss. The poem that follows, "In Memory of," is a private lament for this lost father.

i'm a little late
with mourning
i've been saving you up
for a private ritual,
losing you here and there, now
i remember you in bits (*Circular* 36)

This elegiac note continues in the other poems, "My Mother Has a Photograph," and "The House Where I was Born," which try to recall the fleeting happiness of former times before the war and when the poet was born. But the most moving poem is to his dead brother, "Giorgino Buon Anima," whose name he also bears. Killed at age thirteen by a wayward shell, his enlarged picture is above the kitchen table and his tragic death is retold by their grieving mother over and over again:

> sleep well outside my mother's skull:
> i will leave you alone after her.
> when i am gone
> you will have your name back
> despite me (42)

In many later poems from *The Tough Romance*, Di Cicco retells these war time events from his family history. In "Grandfather" the old man is killed by Nazis; in "Donna Italiana" we have, "my brother's corpse in the shelled house in Arezzo." These scars are always visible to this poet and to the post-war generation who responded to his verse. One of the most recurrent images in Di Cicco's early verse is the remembrance of the dead in the family and in the community. "They are my grandfathers and my great-grandfathers/ and the ancient men that kept my ribs burning at Monte Cassino... "(68) This poet has a profound mission to search for a sense of community among Italians in Canada and to unite them with their relatives in Italy. His own sense of alienation can only be alleviated if he fulfills his poetic quest. This search for a sense of community after the fragmentation of uprooting whole villages is a value he shares with several other Italian-Canadian writers: Dino Minni, Frank Paci, Caterina Edwards, Marco Micone and Pasquale Verdicchio.

In several series of poems, Di Cicco has transformed personal history into works of literature which are moving and powerful. His individual voice is clear; his command of the English language is sure, so sure that he can insert Italian words.

Italian Words

We had all studied English poetry in school and had memorized stanza after stanza of Wordsworth or Tennyson. Shakespeare had given us a sense of speaking the English sentence. In the 1960s we began to read English Canadian poetry which often seemed like American poetry or an imitation of British verse. There were few non-English words, even French words, in Canadian poems. So we were shocked to find Di Cicco's English poems sprinkled with foreign words. But these foreign words were not so foreign to us since they were Italian words from our other life. We first note these strange words in titles of poems in *The Circular Dark*, "La Gente," "il Professore," "Fotografia," and "Giorgino Buon Anima." Di Cicco is slowly changing our understanding of English Canadian poetry. It can no longer be only in pure English. In "Italy, 1974" the opening words, "nella campagna," make us stop and reread this poem. These Italian words are not in these poems for exoticism or for local colour. These are not tourist poems from the voyeuristic gaze of a visitor. These words are used in a very personal manner.

In *A Burning Patience* and in *Dancing in the House of Cards*, there are many Italian words in the titles and in the poems: "Primavera," "Basta," "Rabbia," "Ricordo," "Pietà," "Passato: Love," "I Poeti," "Peccato" and "Ritratto." The repeated and intermittent use of Italian titles gives these words a substance that makes them concrete objects in themselves. Mary di Michele observed that these Italian words act like stones on the smooth English road. (1986)

These Italian words have several functions which can add other levels of meaning to the poems. Sometimes they are used because there is no English equivalent. They reflect the limitations of the new language and of translation. In the case of Di Cicco, we could try to apply the four levels of language described by Henri Gobard, but it would not fit the model in the same way as other Italian-Canadian poets who grew up speaking a regional Italian dialect rather that the official language. Since Di Cicco is from Tuscany, his regional language is also the national language. While growing up, Di Cicco had only two languages to deal with: standard Italian and English. Many of his Italian peers also had one or two regional dialects to contend with which may have put them at a further disadvantage, a situation described by Antonio D'Alfonso in *The Other Shore*. Since Di Cicco escaped this linguistic fragmentation experienced by immigrants from other parts of Italy, he was better able to exercise a leadership role in the development of Italian-Canadian writing.

For Di Cicco, the use of Italian in titles and in poems has an aesthetic function necessary for his type of poetry and for his individual voice. The poet, the speaker, seems to naturally fall back into Italian when the English words fail to capture the full meaning intended. The associations around the word are best communicated in the original Italian term. For example, "Ricordo," a memory, has many associations: remembering a dead family member, having a physical reminder of someone absent, capturing an aspect of nostalgia, making a link to Italy, or as Di Cicco phrases it, "Memento d'Italia." It is a word often used in Italian songs and poetry and this intertexuality is also brought into the English verse. In the poem, "The Statue of Guido Monaco, Arezzo," he articulates some of these cultural memories:

> piazza guido monaco
> and I love each other
> Guido's stone hands
> touch the hills
> into the rivers of dusk (*We are the Light* 13)

While a few of the words are common concrete terms, "piazza," "fotografia," most are abstract words which capture ideas associated with life in Italy, or in Italian culture. "Primavera," literally, first buds, translates as springtime, but it powerfully connotes the early spring of Italy and all the associations with Italian flowers and fruit, with poetry, paintings and music which use the title, "primavera." A number of dishes use the word *primavera* so we also have the aromas and taste of Italian food. Some words have double meanings. "Peccato," means sin, but is also an expression of regret as in "That is too bad." In the poem by that name the speaker expresses regret at the situation he finds himself in and wishes he could escape to a country reminiscent of Italy. "Pietà," meaning pity, is the title of a number of Renaissance paintings and sculptures and has also come to be used in love poetry. However, it also has religious connotations and thus has associations with a mythic level of language. For the poem, "Pietà," it is used in a playful parody of these common places. (*Dancing*, 63) "Ritratto" means portrait, but the word comes from *ritrarre*, to turn away, and the poem gives us a view of the speaker dejected, turned away from the world. It is a measure of Di Cicco's sophistication with two languages that he can play with irony in both in the same work. In many later poems by Di Cicco, the Italian words become more common and more complex, "Nostalgia," "Memento d'Italia," "Maledetto," and "Donna Italiana," all from *The Tough Romance* (1979).

These Italian words evoke the mythic sense of language because they point to a lost language, lost for a whole generation of immigrant children who grew up having to cast aside their regional dialects and learn English as quickly as possible. As a result, a whole emotional level of language has not been open to these people from the time they finished grade school. Di Cicco, even while alluding to these school traumas, tries to recapture this lost language for a whole generation. By strategically placing the Italian word in the English context, he reminds us of those emotional ties to our speech. In this style he has parallels in the poems of Mary di Michele and Antonio D'Alfonso.

To many readers, the function of the Italian words is to remind us that each poem is the work of a writer with that background and is the product of the influence of that distinct culture on the English language poem, making it a poem unlike other Canadian poems. While there is artistic intention in the strategic placement of the Italian words, there is also a strong compulsion to use them. These Italian words may act as stones on the smooth English road but they also add to the pleasing sound of the poetry. The musicality of the Italian language becomes part of the English poem:

> Italia bella; I return to you.
> there is no question of lateness
> for I was taken from you and cannot
> remember the parting. (*Burning*, 25)

Style

There is a discernible difference between Di Cicco's early poetry and his later verse in terms of style, especially in line length and complexity. The style of Di Cicco's early poems is lyrical with a tendency to use the shorter line and smaller stanzas. This is very clear in his first chapbook, *We Are the Light Turning*, which uses a simple, almost child-like, vocabulary and sentence structure:

> The simple words, are they not beautiful?
> The way you hold them up to the light,
> what are they saying?
> Do you recognize it?
> They say the word for light, not
> much more. (11)

The early poems of *The Circular Dark* tend to focus on concrete images, if not concrete objects: an old photograph, an old man, a garden, an old house, a beach, a street at night, a school yard. The language and images can often be impressionistic, capturing a mood or passing emotion, a reaction to a place or event. The images are often metaphors, metonymy, for a life experience or memory. There is a certain power in this stark and minimalist verse. Many poems omit punctuation and focus on word and white space.

Amprimoz and Viselli are correct in observing that "in the case of Italian-Canadian poetry, the experience of language is more important than the language experience." (108)

In contrast to this early verse, Di Cicco's later poetry tends to use longer lines and much enjambment. These are generally longer poems with larger stanzas. They gradually acquire a more abstract vocabulary as the subject matter becomes more overtly philosophical and spiritual. It is now necessary to explain the ideas with more words, rather that just with an impressionistic image. This is epitomized in *Virgin Science*, Di Cicco's last book from the 1980s which includes long prose poems, much repetition, and a mechanistic word play to parody computer and scientific language. There is less use of Italian words; however, many Latin words appear in keeping with the philosophical subject matter and argument.

In *Virgin Science*, Di Cicco is moving on to the intellectual mainstream of academic poetry after having worked through his earlier sense of displacement; a natural evolutionary process. But the legacy that he has given Italian-Canadian writing is in those early works where he traced the transition between two worlds. He was trying to create a sense of community among a lost generation of immigrant children and their parents. The power and purity of Di Cicco's early poems make us return to them over and over again. They deal with honest emotions which we can all appreciate, if not identify in our own experience. For me these qualities are captured in a poem first printed in *Roman Candles*, "The Man Called Beppino":

The man who lost his barbershop during the war
loves great white roses at the back of a house beside
a highway. The roses dream with him,
of being understood in clear english, or of a large
Italian sun, or of walking forever on a
Sunday afternoon. (11)

Notes

Immigrant ships. Passenger ships of the Italian Line that most commonly sailed between Genoa, Naples, Halifax and New York were *S.S. Saturnia* (1946-65), *S.S. Vulcania* (1947-65), *S.S. Conte Biancamano* (1947-60) and the new *Andrea Doria* (1953-56).

The *S.S. Andrea Doria* collided with the *M.S. Stockholm* in a fog bank on July 25, 1956 and sank the next day. There were 1,660 passengers and crew rescued, while 46 people died. Many of the dead were immigrants who drowned in the lower decks.

Immigrant songs. There were many songs on the subject of emigration from Italy. But many songs on nostalgia became immigrant songs due to the hundreds of thousands of people who left Italy. In the minds of these people the lyrics reflected the feelings of the departing emigrant. Titles include "Mamma," by Ferruccio Taglivini, "Papaveri e Papere," by Nilla Pizzi, "Luna Rossa," "La Vigna," " Mamma sei tanto felice," and "La Campagnola," The song

"Caruso," (1986) by Lucio Dalla reverts back to this tradition of immigrant songs even as it has become one of the most recorded songs of the last century.

Works Cited

Amprimoz, Alexandre & Sante Viselli (1985) "Death Between Two Cultures: Italian-Canadian Poetry," in *Contrasts: Comparative Essays on Italian-Canadian Writing*. ed. J. Pivato. Montreal: Guernica Editions.

Blodgett, E.D. (1995) "Towards an Ethnic Style," *Canadian Review of Comparative Literature* 22, 3-4, 623-637.

D'Alfonso, Antonio (1985) *The Other Shore*. Montreal: Guernica Editions.

Di Cicco, Pier Giorgio (1975) *We Are the Light Turning*. Toronto: Missing Link Press.

_____ (1977) *The Sad Facts*. Fiddlehead

_____ (1977) *The Circular Dark*. Ottawa: Borealis Press.

_____ (1977) *Dancing in the House of Cards*. Toronto: Three Trees Press.

_____ (1978) *A Burning Patience*. Ottawa: Borealis Press.

_____ ed. (1978) *Roman Candles: An Anthology of 17 Italo-Canadian Poets*. Toronto: Hounslow Press.

_____ (1979) *The Tough Romance*. Toronto: McClelland and Stewart.

_____ (1986) *Virgin Science: Hunting Holistic Paradigms*. Toronto: McClelland and Stewart.

Di Michele, Mary (1986) Discussion Paper, First National Conference of Italian-Canadian Writers. Vancouver.

Dreadnaught 52, pickup 11 (1976).

Gobard, Henri (1976) *L'Aliénation linguistique*. Paris: Flammarion.

The Grad Post (1976), University of Toronto, 15 April, 1976.

Pivato, Joseph. "Oral Roots of Italian-Canadian Writing," *Echo: Essays on Other Literatures*. Toronto: Guernica, 1994.

Purdy, Al. ed. (1976) *Storm Warning II*. Toronto: McClelland and Stewart.

Living Inside the Poem

MARY DI MICHELE

1. Portrait of the Artist in "A Straw Hat for Everything"

He was lanky and dark, bearded, smoky eyed, and when he spoke it always seemed as if after a long inhalation, the words, on fire. He was lanky and dark, his cords looked slept in, his eyes never, his eyes had the wary alertness of restless nights. He was tall and dark and buff. The black leather of his jacket strained at the shoulders, the pants were gray wool with sharpness at the crease. His hair was closely clipped, his face, shaved to shining. He walked the walk, that mean-streets strut.

He is lanky and dark, he walks with a cane. Although I've never seen him in it, there is a clerical collar that goes with his clothes. But then I live in Montreal, far away from his country parish in King City, Ontario, a town just north east of Toronto, where Pier Giorgio Di Cicco, poet, now also the pastor known as Father

George, enjoys a view of sheep from his garden. He calls himself "content." Content. I used to think that contentment was a poor country cousin to happiness. But in a world, in a language, that is not perfect, "content" is perhaps "as good as it gets."

It has been nearly two decades since those café nights which the layman, my Giorgio, presided over, those nights when he raised conversation to another form of art. On College Street, on St. Clair, on Davenport, on Bloor St. near Spadina – this list is far from exhaustive – where the coffee was Italian and always good. Now we rarely talk and when we do it's over long-distance lines. Still, when I pick up the phone, if he answers, the voice is the one I know, the one that resonates with song, dirge-like in its depth. Perhaps his liturgical practice enhances that soulful timbre in his speech. Otherwise, how does he do it? Smoke, and yet speak through the yogic breath? His words seem to come from deep within him. They've been touched by the heart. But that doesn't mean his language is all sweetness; no, the language never loses its edge. Savour the bittersweet, the *Dolce Amaro*. His words are not *bonbons*, but *bons mots*; wit cuts the sticky sentimentality that "touched by the heart," my own unforgivable cliché, suggests here.

2. How Pier Giorgio Di Cicco Changed my Life

Where does a writer, the poet, begin? It's not ontological, it's not the question "to be or not to be" a writer that interests me, but rather the problem of envisioning, not the role, but the space in language itself. To describe this space is almost as difficult as finding then entering it. I had to coin a word for myself, *langscape*, created by splicing the words, "landscape" and "language," those two figures which shape so much of our sense of identity, both cultural and organic.

This piece, what I'm writing here, is part memoir, part rereading the poetry of Pier Giorgio Di Cicco, through one book, his first major collection, *The Tough Romance*, published by McClelland and Stewart in 1979. (All quotations are from this edition.)

We were introduced in Toronto by the B.C. based poet, Tom Wayman, who, at the time, was writer-in-residence at the University of Windsor. I met Wayman in Windsor where I had been hanging around campus after graduation, returned there after an aborted attempt at a Ph.D. elsewhere. Windsor was then my only link to my aspiration to write: one creative writing workshop, a degree, M.A. in English and Creative Writing, and the $50 award for the best creative writing thesis produced at the university in 1974. That was the slim affirmation I clung to.

My teacher had been the American writer, Joyce Carol Oates, who tried to show me what I hadn't learned in all my advanced literature studies at the University of Toronto yet I desperately needed to know: that there is a profound connection, if not a direct and literal one, between writing and one's life. Sometimes you need Kafka's axe to chop through the ice, the surface of things, to the deeper water, and chop you must, even though this ice may be your family – or your own skin. And what's in those depths, that water? Something living, something brought back from the dead, something both real and dreamed.

That was the hardest lesson I never learned at school about writing. After all, my training had been formally academic; I was taught literature, not writing. Writing's messier, bloody, hard to corral. Literature, that's beef, the name changed from that of the animal, sanitized, indeed, sanctified, the karma dissipated in the meat-making process. What I hadn't understood, but retained, from Joyce Carol Oates' class, Pier Giorgio Di Cicco helped me to see. Now I can smell the difference.

Tom Wayman, a generous and energetic man, bore a striking physical resemblance to Giorgio at the time. Sure Wayman was shorter and a little older, but the dark hair and eyes, the wire-rimmed spectacles, the scruffy beard of the beat poet, the sartorial style, if not the writing, was very similar. What does this serve except to add to some physical sense of the time? The mid-1970s was the sowing time for many of Giorgio's songs, his "post-sixties nocturnes."

Wayman was kind and encouraging to me. He published one of my poems (my first publication!) in an anthology of poems about working, *A Government Job at Last!*, that he was editing at the time. My poem talked about the substitute teaching I had been doing in the local high schools in Windsor, or rather, failing to do. When the principal found me reading during the study period, insouciant to the spitballs flying across the room, I was not asked to "teach" for them again. I needed gainful employment and Toronto was my home, so I soon moved back there. When I did, Giorgio was working on collecting poems for *Roman Candles*, the first anthology of poems written by Italo-Canadian poets to be published.

Reading Giorgio's poems about family, hearing Italian words used freely in the English poem, I found myself responding deeply, and in another way, to poetry. In reading, as in the writing I started to do myself using Italian words, I began to break through to what had been, until then, hidden places in the language. My mother tongue, Italian, and along with it the early childhood experience encoded in it, had drawn no resonances from the pages of the English poetry which had intellectually shaped me. Suddenly those pages opened in a new way. I was able to leave the lobby of literature and approach that entrance leading to real writing. If I fumbled with the knob, no matter, the door opened anyway because Giorgio had jimmied the lock before me.

3. Living Inside the Poem

How do I justify reading life through the poetry, poetry through life? In an interview, part of the documentary film, *That's Why I'm Talking*, Giorgio describes the relationship of his life to his poetry as inseparable. "Everything, even what I had for breakfast, goes into the poem." His poetry embodied his life; it was part song, part sinew.

So I understand Giorgio's sense of living inside the poem – not as inhabiting a house – but as breathing in the body. Poetry is not merely for reading, poetry is for reaching. A "love affair" with Giorgio was like a visit to the tattoo parlour, a passion written on the body.

When he wrote love poetry, which he did in those early days, Giorgio did not write conventional love poetry, but a poetry that sought to be love itself: "a love, which is a poem." In a kind of inverse incarnation, the friends become the poem. (Or this might be better characterized as an "assumption" of the body into the realm of the text.) Giorgio's way in love, in words, is to bring the beloved into the other dimension that is the poem, into a universe field of the poem where the imperative "stay as you are" might possibly be fulfilled.

4. *Langscape*

In opening a space in English language poetry for experience and feeling born in Italian, Di Cicco changed my life and many lives, as well as Canadian literature's langscape. He broke new ground. I followed. "Remembering Baltimore, Arezzo," "The Man Called Beppino," "The First Partita," "Maledetto," "Credo," "Gioventu," "Ecco," "Errore," "Il Tempo," "Nostalgia," "Memento d'Italia," "Ragione," "Mattina," "Donna Italiana," "Toronto-Arezzo," "Aquila," "Canzone,"

"Passaggio," "In Amicizia" and "Voce di Luna": of the eighty-six poems in *The Tough Romance*, twenty use Italian words or place names in the titles. "Remembering Baltimore," "Arezzo" and "Toronto-Arezzo" link disparate cities. Seismic forces are at work in this language where continents, once thrust apart, are drawn together again.

But these connections are made without destruction, without deconstruction; they are realized through a shift in focus on the language, though a kind of 4-D vision. Words found in both English and Italian (those derived from Italian), create a common linguistic space on which to stand. "Nostalgia" is one title where Italian and English are linked seamlessly (no hyphens showing!). I look up "nostalgia" on the English side of my Italian-English dictionary and it gives me "Nostalgia f."; the word loses its gender in an otherwise exact replication in both languages. (This is found under a column headed "nosegay" – what could sound more English, and what less so than its translation *mazzolino di fiori*?) "Nostalgia," what resonates most in this word is not what it means – it means the same in both languages – but its effect/affect. In this English-language poem, the word recalls its buried Latin origin. But what contributes to the 4-D effect on language is time, the history or etymology of words which, I think, works on a sub-liminal level. This history recalls the Latin roots in words we use. Although often obscured or hidden in common language, this heritage is rendered liminal through the poet's bifurcated language.

What does the word, "nostalgia," mean to Di Cicco who, in the closing lines of this poem, finds himself "a little marvellous, with the sunken/ heart of exiles"? The poet has been watching snow falling over the great lake, suffering the cold when he is "obsessed with warmth," imagining "the Tuscan hillsides, pines,/ and the green lizards basking beside the/ cathedral," while shivering before his view of Toronto's winter skyline. There is a dream here, it is his father's dream, and the poem's dream:

> Under a few cold lilies, my father dreams
> cicadas in Vallemaio. I am sure of it.
> He left me that, and a poem that is only a
> dream of cicadas. (*Tough Romance* 48)

This is one man's dream, but that dream is part of a collective one, the dream of a newly found land with its "streets of gold," the dream of "a new world."

What might be the effect of Italian titles, untranslated, on poems otherwise written entirely in English? The Italian words act as markers, as gravestones, pointing to what is buried, but not dead, beneath the surface of the language of the poem. Like many of the figures in the paintings of Leonardo da Vinci, they point to another dimension, another existence. This submerged matrix of Italian language and experience creates a kind of depth of field in the English poem.

Besides the formal and structural work done through the dual languages deployed in the poem, which, thus far, I have attempted to explain in visual terms, there is also a fundamental rupture encountered in language itself. The stress in Di Cicco's poetry, both the vocal and semantic tensions, is on every level of language, from "gibbering" to "song."

There's a basic distrust of language: "the language will trick the mouth into saying he loves." Poetic language seems to offer transformation in that its language of Romance is a language of the body, "the soft rose of the flesh," of the sensuality of flowers, and the poet is fluent in this language: "When I speak roses in fact emerge, roses we take/ shelter in." Who in naming, in merely calling out the name of the dead, the Lazarus, can bring him back? The poet writes "rose" and finds there are petals between the pages! Nevertheless he continues to be not entirely comfortable in this "shelter" offered by a pastoral poetics. He is a twenty-first century man. Although the rift between sign and signifier might seem "healed" in Christian metaphysics, semiotic idealism reverses the process. Where "flesh" is only a word, the world is rendered virtual. In the field of the deconstructed text, shelter can only be a "house of cards."

The poet feels betrayed by this virtual reality, by this language, by the so-called truth of books: "This is cosy, and we have read somewhere that/ this is happiness, except for my wooden legs." Loss through amputation is the image here. The body is displaced, and the legs are replaced by a prosthesis, unfeeling, "wooden." Might language itself be a form of prosthesis? And how might translation impinge on the fit?

Language as displacement is an overt part of the immigrant experience. In the poem, "October Montreal," store names, "Toscana Furniture" and a bust of Dante on Dante Street are Italian signs in a Canadian city, familiar beacons which lured Di Cicco's father to settle with the family in Montreal. It's Quebec, pre-Bill 101, the language law which requires that all public signs be in French. Not that "Toscana Mobilier" would have likely been any more or less familiar to him. What is of note here is the extent to which public signs and place names create *langscape* in a literal way.

Returning to the city twenty-five years later, the poet recalls the isolation of the unofficial language speaker; "the handhold of all those who are lost in their own/ language" (33). In this city of three languages, the poet must find his way:

> ... I walk towards the town,
> the sky on three sides of my brain, in between I am learning a new
> language, always a new language. (33)

There's not a sense of adventure in this "new"; there's a sense of fatigue: "I am sick of/ my lungs."

Language that diminishes, language that turns the body into meat: "my mother, whose bad/ englishes make mincemeat of my will to live." This is an example of language as deeper (I would venture to say) than the defamiliarization of Russian structuralism; this is an example of language as both displacement and disenfranchisement which may be the lot of immigrants, women, racial minorities, all those marginalized through the dictionary. And let us not forget the poor who are currently defined negatively as the "homeless," named by what they don't possess. Di Cicco destabilizes the poetic language he cannot help but sing. He debunks poetry's "uses." "This is the consolation of writing verse./ The academic thimble." The man who speaks roses also experiences language as volatile: "the blue crammed into his mouth like so much dynamite."

A profound ambivalence undercuts the Romantic lyricism in Di Cicco's work. It makes the romance in his writing "tough." The title of this collection links the adjective, "tough," Old English in its source, with the noun, "romance," which is Latin in its origins. The old English word has a visceral quality, the Latinate word is abstract. "Tough" takes a single and heavy stress, while "romance" opens with a lighter note. The former word is a drum, the latter, a piano.

As it approaches oxymoron and contradiction in terms of meaning, the yoking together of the words "tough" and "romance" also creates dissonance in terms of music. This is something of what pushes Di Cicco's romantic lyrics into postmodern irony. Moreover, he deliberately mixes high and low levels of language; poetic, elevated diction is combined with slang or idiomatic phrases in "Canzone":

> ...a way of touching the rose
> in the lover's hand, without telling him the hairs
> of that peachy
> world, his heart, are burning. (79)

Or in "Mattina":

I'm not the wild son-of-a-gun that made your
arms out to be wreathes, out of which happiness
popped its ugly
head, that happiness that hit the roof, the clouds; did
it hit
anything? (53)

What pushes these poems well beyond the
"maudlin," that the poet both embraces and
despairs of, is the way Di Cicco deploys this kind
of linguistic irony. The tall and fantastic figures
of Romance, "This is the effort of giants," are
undercut by the comic, the trifle, "of small furry
things." The laconic "peachy" is paired with the
sacred image of the burning heart.

Yet, unlike the postmodern, Di Cicco's irony
is not disengaged, not cynical, nor does he
disown his own feelings in "Remembering Baltimore, Arezzo":

I am not alone, I have never been alone. Ghosts are
barking
in my eyes, their soft tears washing us down to
Baltimore, out the Chesapeake, round the Atlantic,
round the world,
back where we started from, a small town in the
shade of cypress, with nowhere to go but be still
again.
It is a way of saying twenty-five years
and some German bombs have made for roses in a
backyard that
we cry over, like some film which is too maudlin to
pity

and yet is the best we have to feel human about. (10)

Yes, language both fails and betrays, and sentiment is cheap, but in a world where "The Man Called Beppino," (11) Di Cicco's father, works "for peanuts," what's left over except perhaps the price of admission to some B grade film? The dream of America is compromised: "roses in a backyard" follow in the wake of "German bombs." There is a complex critique here, a judgment made from which the poet does not exclude himself. Di Cicco does not pretend to postmodern, nor modernist, anonymity, but the suffering is also not that of the Romantic poet's "alone." The tears of the audience in the dark theatre are also the poet's tears and "the best we have to feel human about." This quality of feeling is communal; he feels "human" in and through relationships with others. So defined, humanness (to use Di Cicco's noun from the subtitle of his collection *Dark to Light, Reasons for Humanness*) is more important than the aesthetic values which are nevertheless acknowledged to be impaired: "some film which is too maudlin to pity."(10)

5. The Measure of a Man

I admire the size of the heart in Di Cicco's poetry, "my heart has grown double the size of this city." The world is dwarfed by the largeness of the feeling " ...and the Atlantic/ is not big enough for a thimble." (55)

As much as singing is central in the life of the poet – "How many ways does a man/ want to die, or sing or dance or take his pants off?" – it is small when compared with the heart.

The poet is a "chatterbox," the song is "a nutshell," the song "tastes of dust," the song is limited, "There is no song beyond these four walls, the breath." This song is like the maudlin film "not worth our pity" yet attempts to trace, to map, our existence, "this thimble/ our thing, what we've got left to hold on to, this/ motley landscape of who it is we've been... " (23)

Thimble is a recurring image in this collection. It's a homely, homey image; I see a woman's head, bent over her sewing, the thimble, which protects the finger from the sharpness of the needle, gleams in the light from the hearth. The image tempers, in my reading, Di Cicco's critique of language. His is not an attack on language, not a radical deconstruction, but a chiding: there is care in the critique. The poet loves language too much to use the cane. He saves what he can, in art, as in life. He makes do. Truly, tenderly, deeply. There is so much tenderness in this book, it is not neutralized, not undercut. Spatially, the ironic contradictions in the poetry form a kind of vortex.

The concatenation of word and flesh, of writing and life, if this too might be called irony, might best be identified, borrowing from Milan Kundera, as "transubstantial irony." The Eucharist is believed by Catholics to exist at once as both bread and wine and the body and blood of Christ. (A state where the referential fallacy is moot, the metaphoric literal.) Kundera's term seems particularly apt to epitomize Di Cicco's form of irony, for the Catholic priest in him. The language moves through irony and into paradox: a way of saying in language what cannot be, or has not been yet, expressed in words. Because of the limitations of language, the poet has to lay the ground under his feet before he can walk at all. This paradox, like the trope of silence in modern poetics, is one of the topoi of inadequacy which has both fascinated and haunted our age.

6. *Revisiting the scene ten years later*

Since I wrote the sections of the essay above which you have just read, I have moved in different directions only to find myself returning to the poems of Di Cicco and my Italian roots. My novel *Tenor of Love* on the life of Enrico Caruso took me into the early 1900s when many Italians were leaving their towns and villages, much as Caruso did, to seek better opportunities in the New World. The ambivalences that Di Cicco articulated in the preface of *Roman Candles* I found Caruso personified in his yearly movement back and forth between Italy and New York. I have called Caruso our spiritual godfather.

Some of our immigrant parents also returned to Italy only to find that they belonged, ever so tangentially, in Canada. My father moved back and forth several times. In Italy he lamented that it was as if he had not been born in the country; while in Canada he longed for his native land. I too have returned to Italy several times in recent years to work on writing projects and find my inspiration there. I found a deeper connection to German language poet, Rilke, through landscape, the elegies he wrote in a castle in Duino. My current project, an exploration of Pier Paolo Pasolini's poetry, has led me to questions about the different languages in Italy. Pasolini also wrote in the language of his mother, Friulano. And my connection to Italy and Italian is really through the Abruzzese dialect. In Canada, we have been asking what effects a minority language has on an author's English language writing. I once said that the occasional Italian words found in our English poems act like stones on the smooth highway to remind the reader that there is another language and culture behind the work. So, like Pasolini and Di Cicco, I am still trying to deal with the paradoxes and limitations of our languages.

To Speak For, To Write To
*Towards an Expression of our Singular
Being-in-Common in the Poetry
of Pier Giorgio Di Cicco*

> I have this fantasy that he'll betray everything like a
> blubbering infant twenty years from now, as if one
> could hoard up language like finale or a start.
>
> From "Nameless,"
> *Flying Deeper into the Century*

The first time I encountered Pier Giorgio Di
Cicco's poetry I was 15 – the year, 1985. On the
merits of a few heart-felt lines I had written after
the death of a classmate's father, I was chosen by
my high school English teacher (along with some
other friends) to attend a two-day student-
writing conference in Kingston. As it turned out,
something of a Who's Who of Ontario's new
Canadian writers had been assembled to lead
workshops for the students, including Di Cicco.
After the first day, each gave a reading. Di Cicco
read mostly from his book *Flying Deeper into
the Century* (1982), including the poems "Six-
ties Music," "Relationships," "Watching TV,"

"Male Rage Poem" and a new piece called "Brain Litany." I remember because the impression was instant and indelible. Here was a perfect contrast to all the other writers. A poet as one had always imagined, larger than life, with a classical look and an irrepressible politics borne of things any kid could understand: sadness and imagination. There was also his easy entitlement (free of excuse or pride) and his humoured way with the devilish in others. I immediately became a devotee. Over the next year I read *Flying Deeper into the Century* countless times and imitated it shamelessly. A year later, with both of us back at the same conference, I earnestly looked upon Di Cicco as Canada's premier poet. Attempting to engage him as I thought I should – taking my cue from his latest book *Virgin Science* (1986), I feigned familiarity with sub-particle physics, Heisenberg and Bohr, cybernetics and Bateson's double bind. On one occasion, I even found myself violently defending Di Cicco against the suggestion made by another workshop leader that his latest book used faddish science merely to veil a cowardly retreat to religion. It makes me laugh to think of it now, but it was probably the best thing for both of us that Di Cicco subsequently dropped out of the poetry world. My enthusiasms turned elsewhere (again and again). By the time Di

Cicco re-emerged as a poet-priest, I was 31, living in Japan, loyal now to the verse of Ishikawa Takuboku. Which brings me to the crux of this essay. I am here, writing these words, organizing these thoughts, these observations, on this author, not because I possess some incidental expertise. I am not an academic, nor a book critic. I do write poems, but my interest is not to "use" Di Cicco to promote some idea of poetry, his or mine. This is an experiment in attending to the irreducible accident of touch that predicates our being-in-common. More importantly still, in this regard, I seek to follow Di Cicco's lead. Let me explain.

In his "Afterword" to Di Cicco's *Living In Paradise: New and Selected Poems* (2001), Dennis Lee tackles head-on two questions facing any reader familiar with Di Cicco's poetry, who might now, despite a 15-year silence and Di Cicco's supposed re-invention as a Catholic priest, be open to new work. How do we assess his legacy so far? And must we or can we see him with new eyes? Regarding the first question, Lee lays down the basics. The best poems of Di Cicco's early career come together in three collections: *Tough Romance* (1978), *Flying Deeper in the Century* (1982) and *Virgin Science* (1986), each of which exhibit markedly "dissimilar kinds of excellence" (147). Beyond this, Lee is less informative. Following a convention one sees all to often today in poetry reviews and publishing promos, Lee champions Di Cicco's poetry chiefly for its energy: its "gusto," "swagger," "brio," "over-the-top panache," its "pyrotechnics," "break neck trajectories," "amplitude," and of course its "gritty, athletic" and "muscular" lines. In terms often repeated, Lee writes:

> Over and over the poems enact an existential crux: the vital decision to be, to claim the energy of existing now and here ... a Di Cicco poem not only celebrates, it enacts the dynamic force that makes the world go round. (154)

The trouble is that a poem's supposed "energy" can never be accurately measured or separated from the reader's experience. It is too general and too subjective a frame to say anything of consequence about the poems. Similarly, though Lee maintains that there are striking differences between Di Cicco books, his stress on Di Cicco's vitality limits a definition of those very differences. As Lee writes: "All we can say [of each new book] is that he renders the yearning for some larger, more intense life with tingling urgency" (155). As for the question about how we might approach the new poet-priest, Lee is at least more honestly uncertain. Of course, he is in a difficult position. Though a friend and admirer of the Italian-born poet, he has no taste for Christian theology. Nor is he rightfully comfortable depending on a handful of recent poems and Di Cicco's word to steer him right. Still, Lee invites distrust when he quite enthusiastically sidesteps the content of the poems to vaguely hail its "music" – not even its prosody, but its "music of beatitude" and contemplation, showing himself more comfortable with empty truths than incomplete ones. I also think that, while it is merely unfortunate that Lee makes several parallels in hindsight between aspects of the early poems and Di Cicco's later religious views, in one case he steps out of line. Insulted by what he calls a "meanness of spirit" and the "preposterous brain static" of the first part of *Virgin Science*, Lee uses the explicit religious content of the latter poems to justify his befuddlement: "Within the movement of the whole book, they [the last, religious poems] complete a journey to a deep, inexplicable serenity" (160-161). Expected – perhaps, a lost opportunity – certainly, but also no way to read Di Cicco's poetry.

On the contrary, out of respect for the seriousness of his tortured first ambitions, as well as the intelligence of Di Cicco's evolving artistic choices, we must explore the spaces between Di Cicco's texts as much as their identifiable styles, pointing to additions, corrections and rearrangements of concrete features to trace Di Cicco's struggle "towards prayer". As for our attitude on Di Cicco becoming a man of the cloth, we must not forsake the poet for the priest, but approach his new life as well as his "silence" from where we stand as critically informed enthusiasts of his art.

This is what I propose to do. Focusing on the expression of Di Cicco's yearning for community beside his distrust of any ideologically imagined "community of belonging," I will show that the poet's progress through *Tough Romance*, *Flying Deeper into the Century* and *Virgin Science* is not some willy-nilly adventure in search of new vitalities or spiritual comforts, but a tortured working-through of this very double bind. Examining, in particular, the way in which Di Cicco constructs the relationship between writer and reader, I will outline the evolution of a poet who at first is compelled to speak *for* the reader – though he understands full well that subjects and communities are always already divided from themselves, citizen/foreigners as he puts it – but who by turns rejects "mythic speech" to write *to* others, addressing the reader while also acknowledging an impassable gap that disrupts and necessitates all communication. In this way, though my approach aims to correct Lee's short sightedness, my main interest is, in fact, to show that Di Cicco's poetry over the years has always sought to deepen and expand the expression of our being-in-common, and to the lengths of exhibiting something of a poststructuralist politics. Finally, skipping ahead fifteen years to the poem "That First Year" from Di Cicco's collection *The Honeymoon Wilderness* (2002), I will show that this project is not lost or abandoned upon Di Cicco's return to poetry but advanced in an albeit limited way befitting a poet/priest.

To this end let me first clarify my terms, starting with "community," our irreducible being-in-common. In his seminal tract, *The Inoperative Community* (1991) – a book which in the early 80s was one of the first to explore some of the political consequences of Derrida's writing, Jean-Luc Nancy advances a simple but very powerful formula to explain our being-in-common: It does not work. That is, in its essence "community" cannot be produced, or made productive. The benefit of this distinction is that it recovers the revolutionary potential of "community" by swerving clear of the destructive, operational way we currently characterize togetherness: on the one hand, as *society* (an economic association based on needs) and on the other as hypostasis – the myth of belonging, of shared blood or ground. Apparently, the weakness of

Nancy's characterization though is that it leaves us helpless. How can we imagine something that is beyond myth and mechanism? How do we act politically and not put our ideals to work? But in fact Nancy gives us lots to go on. The very condition of our being-in-common can be understood, he writes, as a "finitude, or the infinite lack of the infinite identity of community." It can be encouraged (if not forcibly made) "in the retreat or by the subtraction of something" (xxxix); by any act that interrupts relations of need or myths of collectivity and exposes finite relations. For artists specifically: "It is a question of understanding before all else that in 'communication' what takes place is an *exposition*, finite existence exposed to finite existence, co-appearing before it and with it"(xxxix). This paper shares Nancy's perspective. When I speak of our "being-in-common," I mean that horizon of finitude-between-beings which lies beyond "mythic speech" and use, and which requires a retreat from these practices and assumptions to approach. Moreover, when I claim that Di Cicco "has sought to deepen and expand" the expression of community, I mean "deepen" in the sense that he has realized more and more precisely Nancy's view/approach in his work and "expand" in the sense that he has brought more and more of the features of his craft under its influence. In fact, one of the reasons it seems pertinent to me to focus on the development of Di Cicco's relationship to the reader is that it highlights a key but often overlooked (by writers and readers alike) aspect of any poem that eventually comes into line with Di Cicco's instincts. Also, later in the essay I emphasize Di Cicco's acknowledgment of an irreparable gap between writer and reader. This should not be taken to mean that I equate absolute finitude with any fissure or break, or community with any demonstration of difference. I merely stress it to prove a qualitative turning point – Di Cicco's resolve not to "go there," not to speak for others. Finally, I use Nancy's term "mythic speech" as he does to refer to the form, tone and rhetoric of the speaking for others, relating the myth of essential belonging.

So let's turn then to chart the early evolution of Di Cicco's relationship to the implied reader. Beginning with *The Tough Romance*, Di Cicco sets the trend by imagining a reader incidental to his own divided self. In one of the very first poems of the volume, "Birthday Poem to Myself" (7), for example, we find Di Cicco using a second-person address that at times refers directly to himself ("Birthday boy, your day is coming"), and at other times just hangs there, the twisted echo of common poeticism:

"There is not so much love in the whole world/ as what I've saved up for you." The effect is a reader that is called, but who must come through the backdoor on a slippage, the split mirror of his narcissism. Also, the tone and thrust of Di Cicco's address is "mythic speech." Whether you imagine "the other self" to be a lost boyhood Giorgio, an eerily indistinct lover or the vicarious reader, the suggestion is that the poet is speaking *for* the other as if life itself: "I am speaking from your cradle,/ from the far end of your grave. And I speak/ like your own mother" (7). Of course, the inter-subjective relationship between writer and reader is much more open, more co-dependent than that, and Di Cicco knows it. Although at times he seems confident that his romanticized picture of himself as a double agent – and in particular as a citizen/foreigner, following his remarks in his anthology, *Roman Candles* (1978), that "the true citizen remains a foreigner" (10) – is appealing enough to a certain audience to excuse his lofty navel-gazing, at other times he belies his anxiety by prodding the reader into his scheme. Consider the harshness that comes out of nowhere with the last line, "the kick in the/ back of the head." In a bullying gesture more clearly directed to the reader, the poet seems to be saying: In speaking to myself I can either speak

for you or not – it's your loss. But again Di Cicco
understands (consciously or unconsciously) the
problem. Di Cicco encapsulates the limitation of
"mythic speech" in the poem "The Last Aunt"
from this same book. The poem's subject is an
85-year-old aunt, "A fine tired woman, her mind
gone, gibbering lonely/ things"(51). A sad state
for sure, but one Di Cicco pushes towards a
telling tragedy when he adds: "If she is cold, it is
because we tell her so./ If she is tired, it is
because it is time to come in" (51). Isn't this the
same predicament that the reader of *The Tough
Romance* is in – edged by forces out of one's
control into a half-presence that *is* what it is
told? And to be fair things do evolve over the
course of the book. The penultimate poem of
the collection, "Birthday Gathering," for
example, loses the second-person address.
Recounting what happens at the same birthday
that the poet was looking ahead to at the beginning, we find Di Cicco with a more diffuse, less
commanding voice: "A little old we are, and cel-
ebrating/ one of us./ It is my birthday. My turn
rises, falls in their hands, they/ discuss" (100).
The poet is one among friends. And as far as it is
possible to link Di Cicco's apartment to the
page, the poem to its balcony – "All my friends
come to the balcony, come to the balcony" – or
our sense of the lines to "the hard fog/ clogging/

90

the eyes of the skyline" (100), we the reader can count ourselves a friend too. Has Di Cicco's stance towards the reader changed? Not exactly. At best, the poet has morphed from a bully into a passive-aggressive. "I will come back to this place, this night," he writes, "handcuffed in the heart of my friend" (100). You are bound to me as I am to you, it says. You must speak for me now as I've spoken for you.

Where trying to fit oneself into Di Cicco's world in *The Tough Romance* involved all the denial and danger of a bed-trick, reading *Flying Deeper into the Century* is like being swept up into a festival parade – it may not be "you," but it feels like fun and most anyone can join in. In *Flying Deeper into the Century*, though Di Cicco continues to assume the role of a mythic poet speaking *for* the reader, he is able to touch many more readers by adding the context of Reagan era-politics, the long march of yuppie-dom and the ticking information bomb into the mix. The poet's private tortures now seem more like all our problems:

> …We are lucky to be mature,
> in our prime, seeing more treaties, watching
> T.V. get computerized. Death has no dominion.
> It lives off the land. The glow over the hill, from
> the test sites, at night, the whole block of neighbours
> dying of cancer over the next thirty years. We are
> suing the government for a drop of blood; flying

> deeper
> into the century, love,
> the lies are old lies with more imagination;
> the future is a canoe. (16)

Supporting the poet in this regard is an also more "public voice" (as Lee calls it) that retreats from direct address, replacing the pronoun "you" most often with "world" or "love" as in the line "flying deeper/ into the century, love,/ the lies are old lies" (16). The effect is a welcome staginess, artistic distance where there was once the push and pull of a lover's "whatever." The poet also radically complicates his use of "deep images," something that in Canada is associated with Di Cicco and *The Tough Romance*. In his previous collection, the short lyrics often put tremendous weight on a few inexplicable images, repeating some – like "thimble" and "footprints" – from poem to poem with little variation. In *Flying Deeper into the Century*, however, propelled by longer prosaic lines, Di Cicco regularly runs away with an image, extending it as much as he revises it in process. Take, for instance, the last lines from the title poem:

> ...Glumly, glumly, deeper
> I fly into the century, every feather of each wing
> absolution, if only I were less than human, not angry
> like a beaten thing. (16)

92

Daring a paraphrase, one could argue that the poet says here: I live-on ever more an animal. Yet how could this ever do? The pretext is "animal," what Di Cicco derives from the verb "fly" in his refrain "flying deeper into the century," but the animal image, what appears here and then there, cannot be separated from the metonymic action. With the wings (hope and potential) of an eagle, the head (self-dividing knowledge) of a human and the body (pain and thoughtless reflex) of a beast of burden or perhaps caged lion, it is the cinematically posed image of a Grecian sphinx (making it a worthy bookend to Yeats' famous poem) as also what any reader always sees, a seam of the seam of what seems. If one recalls Robert Bly's characterization of "deep image" poetry as a leap into the unknown that should incite the reader's collective unconscious, this amounts to exposing *canto 'roberto' jondo* for its myth of a binding and accessible universality. In line more with Lacan or Zizek, than Jung, Di Cicco suggests that one's sense of the unknown or the surreal is not one's own, but must be interrupted at every turn. All of which not only adds up to more reading to do, and thus more finite space for the reader to be, but the sugges- tion is that already part of Di Cicco's practice is a form of critical reading, levelling the playing field even further. Still, reference to a larger political world and broader definition of reading is a shift in the scope, not kind. Ultimately, the reader of *Flying Deeper into the Century* remains defined by the privileged position Di Cicco again assumes for himself as *the* voice of public outrage. As the poem "On Religious Talk Shows" nicely exemplifies, though our collective stomachs churn when Di Cicco recounts the details of an evangelist's TV spectacle, what the last line shows – what reads, "I didn't mind a lot of it,/ but when they brought Ronald Reagan on and asked him/ how a Christian deals with foreign policy and/ he answered with a straight face – for Christ's sake,/ I puked" (22), by design it will be Di Cicco alone throwing up a poisonous world and into *our* laps.

The true paradigmatic shift in Di Cicco's relationship with the reader occurs in *Virgin Science*, the last book of his early career. Here the poet foregoes "mythic speech" to expose the irreducible impasse that defines the writer and reader's shared being-in-common. In one of the first poems of the first section of the book, "Dying To Myself," Di Cicco more or less announces this change outright when he remarks that his work is *not for* someone, not for the "Protestant brain" (6) and not for a Canadian audience. "I have grown up to be a metaphysician," says Di Cicco in the poem "The Happy Time" and in this "Protestant/ country – they have no talent for metaphysics" (5). Should we deem such statements as "meanness of spirit"? I think base or crude comedy is more apt. Either way, this is a necessary move for Di Cicco. By establishing a limit between himself and the reader – albeit one created in part for shock value and which he himself is not ready to fully commit; "well to be brutal about it," he admits, "it isn't just the Italians that can do this. The obedient heart could do it" (6) – he lays down the conditions for true dialogue, a gap that cannot be traversed by some "myth of belonging" or erased by the pyrotechnics of some mythic songster. "I don't know what I want to ruminate/ of the past, but the guts extend themselves/ by the grace of something other" (5). Also, with this gesture Di Cicco comes clean about a very specific reader that he has always perhaps had in mind, the model Canadian reader, the one he hoped to make into a "citizen/foreigner," but whom (as we have seen) he always distrusted and, likely, never addressed outright for fear of the consequence to his ambitions – if you question the reality or the power of such a reader, remember Lee's reaction. The ghost is now out of the closet and instead of participating in some self-aggrandizing/self-defeating exchange of myth for myth, or employing a double-speak, the way "the English say welcome, when they mean goodbye" (6) to win from the "order of things" some literary freedom, the author now seeks to designate his own world. "An apple is a kiss, a friend is a smile," Di Cicco writes, "and these things are not poetry" (5). It is a (relatively) bold move supported by an even bolder effort in the main, title section of the book. But unfortunately this cannot be the place to do this unique and complex work justice. For those stumped by the text, I suggest taking the section's lead quotes by Charles Hampden-Turner, Michael Talbot and St. Augustine as your map. With these fragments, Di Cicco introduces not only his program but his method: to wage holy war against ideology (specifically, instrumental science, Platonic metaphysics and native poetry) via a *naïve* science of sub-atomic discourse smashing. Take some lines, for instance, from any poem, say, "The Immaterialist: The Magic of Mind over Matter":

> Lovers. The funeral pyre of dualism.
> Idealization as the multi-dimensional
> hologram incarnate.
> He fell off the cross and splintered into locality.
> An arm here, a leg there. Uproarious cumulous laughter.
> Generations of specialists. (69)

Imaginary technologies, Descartes meets Joan-of-Arc, a *Trauerspiel* passion, collage as poetic equation – the whole point here is to create what Lee ridicules as "preposterous brain static"; or more precisely, in the manner of a contemporary baroque, to germinate ruminations. If Di Cicco falters, it is when he doesn't go far enough. "Believing is seeing," reads the next line. "Not a ghost of a chance with her." (69) – though the line's end rhyme with "cumulous laughter" certainly complicates things. As for a sample of how these poems support Di Cicco's newly reoriented relationship with the reader, consider Di Cicco's extensive use of quotes and "ex-postulates" to start off most of the poems of the section. This is not a poet assuming and forcing a vague connection with his reader. On the contrary, the quotes suspend at least two levels of difference between the parties. First, distinct from an inter-subjective relation, the quotes point to what Kristeva terms "intertextuality". All writing is already part of a constellation of other texts in which (in a sense) the writer and reader have already met, the references say. This is where a good portion of any dialogue takes place. Text is paratext; immediacy is elsewhere. Second, by citing specific excerpts from Neils Bohr and Novalis, St. Augustine and Gregory Bateson, Carlos Castaneda and Czezlaw Milosz (to name a few), these references emphasize different finite positions in discourse. If the reader doesn't know anything about cybernetics, autopoiesis or Bateson's idiosyncratic characterization of "mind," the passage by Bateson that begins "The Cybernetic Holist," for example – "...any ongoing ensemble of events and objects which has the appropriate complexity of casual circuits and the appropriate energy relations will surely show mental characteristics" – will mean little. And yet if the reader *does* know what's going on, the reference only helps to differentiate Di Cicco from Bateson. "Haunted houses are residual mind./ Mind you don't trip on the stairs." (95)

So here we have it, a glimpse of Di Cicco's early progress – its zigzag path from speaking *for* community to writing *to* others out of community; from speaking for himself as a model of romantic cosmopolitanism, to speaking up for people against Globalization (as we now understand it), to writing from and to the place of a limited, situated reader.

Before we turn to show how Di Cicco continues to advance this trend, let's consider first Di Cicco's fifteen-year hiatus from publication. Like Dennis Lee, I do not believe that it is the critic's business to judge Di Cicco becoming a priest – obviously. The matter is as plain as it is beside the point. He pursued another career. Still, we should not also let this limit prevent us from asking the question: What does Di Cicco's choice *do* for *the poet*? To do so, in the case of his "silence" for example, would be to give the false impression that "silence" does not also *do* something; that Di Cicco's retreat from writing (in the "proper" public sense) could not also be – like Bartleby's famous abstention – a form of writing itself. In fact, following Nancy, isn't this what we have demonstrated here? By relinquishing "mythic speech" Di Cicco has done more to enrich and complicate his relationship with the reader than anything else. Remember too that Di Cicco is an improvisation artist. His poems are (or come off as) of-the-moment expressions of risk and invention, with his voice, even his *raison d'être* as a poet, up for reinvention from poem to poem. What more elusive, yet necessary, prize is there for such a writer than to improvise poetry's end, or, for that matter, the coming to poetry? To do so is to collapse the very distinction between doing and meaning and to win the ground upon which every improviser exercises their flights of freedom. This promises to be an interesting and essential avenue of questioning for another time. What does giving up poetry *do*? Is there a modern tradition of poetry's renunciation? Can we fit Di Cicco's hiatus beside Rimbaud, Laura Riding and others in this bastard history? Is there a poetics of renunciation? Might such a retreat be incorporated or already at work in literature? For now and for our purposes, it will be enough to simply observe that Di Cicco's new career affords the poet new freedoms with new limits. For one, as we have already suggested, one of the key catalysts driving the Italian-born poet towards a redefinition of our being-in-common (besides his "immigrant" experiences and his unrelenting intelligence) is his sense of the limitations of literary taste and decorum under Canadian cultural nationalism. Joining the Catholic priesthood changes this dramatically. In effect, it guarantees Di Cicco part of what he was always after: both economic and social independence from the rule of the national symbolic. On the other hand, the content of Di Cicco's choice amounts to a lot. As the citizen-cleric of a privileged non-state actor like the Catholic Church, he may have won the license to be something of a purist, but the promise of his earlier trajectory, towards finitude, is greatly limited. To put it mildly, though we might expect Di Cicco to fearlessly exploit all the alchemical conceits of St. Bernard, we can also count on him to remain (in his own words) a "feminist nightmare" – something that should not be overlooked or taken lightly. Still, the wager of this essay is that, even given these limits, Di Cicco stays faithful to advancing an expression of our being-in-common – something which we will see the poet does (not surprisingly) by making do with less.

In the "Preamble" section of Di Cicco's book *The Honeymoon Wilderness* (2002) – his first full-length volume in sixteen years, the poem "That First Year" stands out for a familiar subject: the yearning for community. Here, Di Cicco recounts his struggles to assimilate into the society of Augustinian monks he joined in the mid-80s when he first turned to religious life. I humbled "myself among men who doubted me for having gotten the world's publicity," Di Cicco explains, "what did I want with them, anyway?" (17). As well as he expresses his desire to return faced with a frenetic world: "i get tired now, going downtown, the noise and ruckus of/ portuguese youths blasting and cruising... the traffic money-making rush of decent/ moms and dads in their illusion of house/ and car... I want to go back" (17). Thus again we find the poet still tortured by his longing for community and his belief that it can never be willfully won or guaranteed (since it is easy to believe Di Cicco could go back to the monastery if he wished). And yet with "That First Year" the poet also seems never clearer, direct or at peace with this impasse. Sure, on the surface of things, the new poems read like "heart rambles, head rambles … in an amiable middle gear which is unlike any previous Di Cicco voice" (Lee, 164), but it goes deeper than that. For one, there is no subtext of blame or self-promotion here – no (explicit or implicit) foil made of outside censorship, for instance; or stagy, new poetics that, while promising a better vehicle to exhibit our being-in-common, also sells a "signature" limit. Presumably, Di Cicco said his piece in *Virgin Science* and now the poet/priest lives it, giving up on not only the myth of belonging, but also some productive *uses* of its expressed impossibility. Along these lines, we also find poetry itself serving a diminished and very specific role in Di Cicco's life. Compare, for instance, the description of prayer at the climax of "That First Year" and the act of reading, a parallel supported by the poet's subtle use of line breaks, dashes and ellipsis. "I want to go home," Di Cicco says, speaking of the monastery. "We would just sit together, god and i/ with eyes that penetrated" (18). Though "like all the others I make use of/ his creation and forget – / to wait for him … just wait for him" (18). According to this subtle analogy, both are engagements with an Other, both are exercises in attention, both are culturally situated, embodied acts and both are always incomplete. And yet also for Di Cicco clearly prayer is the more essential practice, the lens through which he now sees the problem of "writing" community as a practice of attending, mediating, *being with*. It is not that Di Cicco's new poetry has *become* prayer, but has now come to exist *beside* prayer as another vehicle of the impossibly intimate and impossibly unflinching relation between oneself and the Other.

And, of course, all of this changes Di Cicco's relationship to the reader. Remember that in *Virgin Science* the poet trumped something of "mythic speech" by acknowledging the gap between writer and reader. It was a crucial step. But one achieved mainly by pushing the reader away, through various alienation effects. With a relative withdrawal from authorial ambition, on the other hand, Di Cicco establishes a similar gap in a less affected way. Still, the genius of "That First Year" is that the poet does not rest on the laurels of his new (albeit compromised) independence as priest. Di Cicco exercises as much poetic talent as he does detachment. With the advantage of stressing both time and the symptomatic body over subject positions abstracted in discursive space, Di Cicco deliberately weights the gap between writer and reader this time through a special kind of paradox – "whatever singularities."

In *The Coming Community* (1990), Giorgio Agamben introduces the two aspects of his term "whatever singularity" this way. First, it is, of course, a singularity; by definition, anything "freed from the false dilemma that obliges knowledge to choose between the ineffability of the individual and the intelligibility of the universal" (1). An aporia among aporias would be one example – what is at once irreducible to universal categories but finite in relation to other related paradoxes. Second, in variance to, say, Derrida, who (famously, but not exclusively) sought to expose singularities behind the transcendental terms of metaphysics, "whatever singularities" arise, says Agamben, from "an original relation to desire," a "*whatever* being":

> The singularity exposed as such is whatever you want, that is, lovable.
> Love is never directed towards this or that property of the loved one (being blond, being small, being tender, being lame), but neither does it neglect the properties in favor of an insipid generality (universal love): The lover wants the loved one with all of its predicates, its being such as it is. (2)

In other words, "whatever singularities" are examples of life and expression that we accept as "irreparable" or approach "as such." What we love, not because it is prudent or irresistible, but because we can.

One way that this kind of paradox shows up in Di Cicco's poem "That First Year" – that is, predicated on the "affectionately finding para-doxical," if you will – is when it is entwined with stylistic gestures from Di Cicco's past career. Take the ironic line: "Men without women can use an Italian/ now and again to laugh christ off the cross and make him dance/ make the devil look a bit foolish" (17). Is this not the Di Cicco of *Tough Romance* risking it all for an unlikely image? Or what about Di Cicco's hot political scorn for "literature taking itself seriously" fitted to the hyperbole, "and anyone/ taking something serious to get away from pointlessness" (17)? Then there is the poet's retreat from poetry proper, as in *Virgin Science*, to prove a larger textual world. "i wrote poems mainly that first year," remarks Di Cicco, ripe with the irony that he hadn't yet arrived. Whereas now:

> i want to see everything as a sign: something
> dropped, a cloud going the
> wrong way; and not in a town where there
> are signs everywhere, and no signs. (17)

True, these echoes are likely symptomatic, habits of thought and expression built up over the years, but the point is that they are here and recast as moments of suspension. We might believe from their inclusion that part of the reason that Di Cicco returned to publication is that he has come to accept the breadth of his early poetry – the whole god-forsaken, vain project of it. Re-exposed via irony and paradox, moreover, Di Cicco now invites the reader to stand with him, *be apart/ with* the irreparable past.

Another place we find "whatever singularities" in "That First Year" is in the poem's precise subtlety, in particular, the many layers of paradoxes that Di Cicco compresses into the climax of the piece:

> ...like you
> i can't be away for far too long; wherever you are,
> waiting,
> in death or hayfields,
> call me "in-free" before dusk. (18)

Perhaps you recognize the use of the second person address from Di Cicco's earlier poems? Or not – a lot has changed. In the past, "you" usually referred to a shamefully absent or blindly hopeful set of candidates. Here it specifies a precise plurality. "You" is himself, god, world, mother, brother and reader, each of which Di Cicco clearly poses as singularities. For example, consider the way god appears in the above passage, "waiting,/ in death, or hayfields." This is no doctrinaire view of omniscience. It is a pic-

106

ture of an elusive pseudo-presence shuttling between what is absolute – that is, like mortality – and what is a fleeting accident of nature, as when a beam of light is cast from clouds onto hayfields, spotted perhaps while driving through Ontario or Italy. Plus, relayed through the hub of this plurality, god is also at once mother, for example – calling us in "before dusk." Added to the built-in paradoxes of Di Cicco's second person address is his demand "call me." In a clever double bind, the suggestion is that what I name you is at the same time how I call *to* "you," so that no matter how you call *to* me, you will name me the same way. Finally, we have the very curious term "in-free" which, Di Cicco says, "you" should call him. Its construction belies the paradox: two words and two uses of punctuation. Two types of signs that divide "the rule" from "the exception" of proper signification, a script from the superscript, text and paratext, and yet which signifies a collapse of these distinctions, an "in-ness" in common and in process. Assuming the words "in" and "free" are self-explanatory in this regard, examine how the dash equally separates and conjoins "in" and "free" or how the quotation marks work. As we have already in effect demonstrated, these quotes are *of* "in-free," *in* the word (if we can call it that). While they suggest a source text in form, in content – because they frame a single and very unlikely prepositional phrase – they only beg further citations, what is impossible since double quotes only open themselves up to more quotes *in absurdum*. A suspension of the terms original and copy, inside and outside, Di Cicco's use of quotations exhibits the paradox of citation's very example. As poignant subtlety, it shows the poet's love of poetry.

Works Cited

Agamben, Giorgio. *The Coming Community*. Vol. 1. Minneapolis: University of Minnesota Press, 1993.

Di Cicco, Pier Giorgio. *Flying Deeper into the Century*. McClelland and Stewart, 1982.

—. *The Honeymoon Wilderness*. Toronto: Mansfield Press, 2002.

—. *Living in Paradise: New and Selected Poems*. Afterword by Dennis Lee. Toronto: Mansfield Press, 2002.

—. *Roman Candles: An Anthology of Poems by Seventeen Italo-Canadian Poets*. Toronto: Hounslow Press, 1978.

—. *Tough Romance*. Reprinted. Guernica Editions Inc., 1990.

—. *Virgin Science*. Toronto: McClelland and Stewart, 1986.

Nancy, Jean-Luc, et al. *The Inoperative Community*. Vol. 76. Minneapolis, MN:

University of Minnesota Press, 1991.

Seeking the Divine

Toronto's Poet Laureate Rediscovers
Prayer Through Poetry

STACEY GIBSON

The hallways of U of T's Department of Italian Studies, like most academic corridors, contains an oppressive stillness. Behind closed doors, professors may be deciphering the allegories of Dante's heaven and hell or ruminating on the writings of Boccaccio, but the main hallway is damp with silence.

This quietude is dissolved – if only for a moment – by Pier Giorgio Di Cicco, Toronto poet laureate and visiting professor of Italian-Canadian Studies at U of T. He is slipping away from his office for a break, and has brought his digital recorder. He hits play, and a recording of 1950's crooner Jerry Vale's "This is the Night" strains through the miniature speaker. "This is the night, it's a beautiful night and we call it bella notte...." He hums happily. An assistant peers guardedly out of her office. "This song reminds me of an Italian restaurant on Mulberry Street in New York that I've never been to," he says. "An Italian restaurant with heaping plates of spaghetti, and a pergola overhead with plastic grapes attached to it."

Outside the building, Di Cicco lights a Matinee king size. He is down from the two-packs-a-day habit of his youth to one pack. ("You can quote me," says his friend, Rector Robert Nusca. "Tell him he's got to stop having five cigarettes for every espresso.") Students scurry past head down, intent on getting to class. From beneath his moss-green brimmed hat, Di Cicco watches them curiously. He notes – in an almost injured tone: "Everybody is always hurrying. Always going somewhere."

It doesn't take much time with Di Cicco to realize that it's not the "going somewhere" he objects to, but the manner of the journey. He believes people need to "see their daily lives as a poem" – and this requires incorporating art and poetry into the business of living. Back in his office, he speaks in the same slightly wounded tone. "Art is not out there. People think it's out there. The creative product is not outside of them. How can they see it, if they don't know it is in here?" he asks pointing to his heart. "If they don't see themselves as writing the poem of their life, their daily life, why should they read a poem?"

It's a mindset he brings to the role of poet

110

laureate of Toronto. In December (2004) during his inaugural speech at Toronto City Hall, he urged a change of attitude – a new way of seeing ourselves and the city – that incorporates the notion of artistry and citizenry into one ethos. "A vibrant urban art teaches the art of life; but if the daily life is not artistic, inspired by intimacy, zest and sociality, the passion is missing, and a city without passion is just a series of artistic events," he said. "Toronto has succeeded at just about everything, except looking glamourous to itself; and by glamour I mean a city's attraction to its own uniqueness, moved by the conviction that there is a style of creativity that can only be done here."

Di Cicco was appointed poet laureate of Toronto – a position of cultural ambassadorship – in September, 2004, and held the post until 2007. He took over from Dennis Lee, Toronto's first poet laureate and the author of such poetry collections as *Un* and *Nightwatch* and the children's classic *Alligator Pie*. By the age of fifty-six, Di Cicco has produced nineteen books of poetry, each one radically divergent in scope and voice. From the powerful neo-surrealist images that first emerge in *A Burning Patience* (1979), to philosophic meditations incorporating science and art in *Virgin Science: Hunting Holistic Paradigms* (1986), to the exploration of spirituality and faith in the *Honeymoon Wilderness* (2002), his work constantly shifts its shape. His collection, *Dead Men of the Fifties* (2004), reveals another departure in voice. With the mirthful energy of a swing dancer and comic timing of Jack Paar, Di Cicco jitterbugs his way through the landscape of the 1950s, casting an eye on Hollywood stars, musicians and the everyday people of the post-war decade.

Like his poetry, Di Cicco's journey is filled with a series of radical turns. He was born in 1949 in Arezzo, Italy, south of Florence, where he lived until the age of three. He has three memories of that time: a palm tree outside the room in which he was born; the billowing waves of the Mediterranean; his grandmother's bouffant hairdo. "All the others are textured memories of the synesthetic kind," he says. "Because when I was a kid, before they taught me Aristotelian senses, I could smell colour, feel music." His father was a barber who played the accordion in dance bands. His mother, a homemaker, sang him arias and love songs.

Before his birth, during the Second World War, his brother was killed in an Allied bombardment in the area between Naples and Cassino. His mellifluous voice turns low and staccato when he speaks of it. "My brother – died – from a shell. I had a brother who I never saw. I think he was thirteen, maybe twelve, when he was caught in the bombing." He takes a deep, cavernous breath and shifts to another subject. His father's barbershop was also levelled during the bombings.

The family, which included an older sister, moved to Canada to rebuild. They lived in Italian communities in Montreal, then Toronto, where, Di Cicco says "the culture remained encased in amber." But that refined Italian ambience was swapped for a steel-town existence when the family moved to Baltimore when he was eight. The city certainly had its graces in the 1960s, but they were of the salty, rugged Eastern Seaboard flavour. Athletics trumped literature. Blue-collar workaday concerns left little room for arias and poetry. Di Cicco adhered to the social climate, excelling at baseball and lifting weights.

At fifteen, he found the book, *The Art of Thinking* on a paperback carrel in a grocery store. Written by Voltairian freethinker Ernest Dimnet, it championed the idea of independent thought. "The idea fascinated me," says Di Cicco. "I had no idea you could have things in your head that would take the place of activities. It started Socratic kinds of dialogue in my head, and got me questioning and becoming philosophical." Shortly after, he stocked up on the poetry of John Keats, Percy Bysshe Shelley and William Wordsworth. He would take his books to the cemetery, sit on the tombstones and read "forever." In the quiet space, he found solace in his readings, in his philosophical musings, and in his inceptive attempts at writing rhymed verse and sonnets.

The immigrant experience may have amplified his talent for precise nuance and rhythm, says Rita Davis, executive director of the culture division at Toronto City Hall and Di Cicco's friend since the 1970s. "I share that immigrant experience. And when you're an immigrant, you learn to – without even noticing it – become extraordinarily sensitive to the signals around you, because you need that for basic survival. Not survival like food and water, but social survival. It's actually an enormously interesting tool later in life, but Giorgio takes it from being a tool to being an art... he understands the powerful effect of language used with precision and care, and the fine attention to the nuance of the word."

At eighteen, Di Cicco left the city of Baltimore behind and moved in with his sister in Toronto. He soon enrolled at Erindale College, immersing himself in the theatre scene – as part of the university's Poculi Ludique Societas, a group of touring medieval and Renaissance players. Di Cicco performed in plays on campuses across North America. He took on roles in other U of T productions, including St. Thomas à Becket in T.S. Eliot's *Murder in the Cathedral*. "I did so much theatre that I failed," he says. "I didn't pay any attention to zoology and botany and whatever else." After enrolling in University College the following year, he stitched together a curriculum composed entirely of poetry courses. He found particular inspiration in Latin American neo-surrealists such as Pablo Neruda, Rafael Alberti and Cesar Vallejo, admiring them for their ability to "practice a brand of neo-surrealism that wasn't off-the-wall surrealism, but was grounded in good imagism – imagism that was netted to the subconscious."

After graduating, Di Cicco continued with his job as a bartender at the Graduate Students' Union pub. After closing up the bar, he would return to his apartment near Spadina and Bloor, and write poetry until the early morning hours. "On Walmer Road in midtown Toronto it's the least noisy time of the day. Three in the morning is just perfect. It's just nighthawks. Just you and the nighthawks and the typewriter." A two-finger typist, he would pound out poems on his Olympia typewriter, emptying bottles of eraser fluid. ("Today's generation can't comprehend the aggravation of having typewriters and eraser fluid," he grumbles. "It was a physical, manual labour of love.")

His poetic output was enormous. After a stint at *Books in Canada*, where he worked his way up from subscription manager to editor, he soon became one of the few people in Canada making a living from poetry-related activities. Within a few years, he had been published in 200 magazines internationally: *Critical Quarterly. Descant. Poetry Australia. Quarry.* He wrote his first collection, *We Are the Light Turning* (1975), in two weeks. He produced enough material for thirteen collections of poems in less than a decade. He edited *Roman Candles*, the first anthology of Italian-Canadian poetry. And then, at the age of thirty-three, he stopped cold. And he wouldn't publish another poem for fifteen years:

> First days. I remember continual tears. Tunnels of lightless light.
> The invigorating blessed air. The clear and prolonged vistas. ("First Days," *Living in Paradise*)

Who can ever truly know what propels a spiritual quest, far from the world one has always inhabited? All that can ever be glimpsed are shadows, perhaps a line or two of poetry, into a private journey. In 1983, Di Cicco arrived at the door of Marylake, an Augustinian monastery outside of Toronto. A prior named Father Cyril opened the door. Di Cicco asked, Have you got any use for a middle-aged literate like me? The father said, Sure, come on in. Put our library in order and do some dishes and pick up some garbage.

As "the low man on the totem pole," Di Cicco washed and dried hundreds of dishes daily and served the thirty residents at every meal. He kept the library tidy. He attended community prayers. He acted as a translator for the largely Italian-speaking groups that made pilgrimages to the grounds on Sundays. His room was a brick cell with only a sink, a bed, a desk. From his window, he admired the "lovely view of a little lake behind the monastery, and a lovely little fountain that hardly ever ran, with our Blessed Mother presiding over the blue waters."

The duties and servitude incumbent on the lowest member in the hierarchy was welcomed by Di Cicco: "It was discipline. And it was in the spirit of service, not in the spirit of 'my rights are being infringed upon.' The smaller you made yourself, the closer you felt to God. So the question of rights and dignity was academic or foolish. Spiritual progress often doesn't rely on rights and questions of autonomy. You don't ask yourself every three minutes whether your sacrifice was worth it."

Di Cicco's shift away from a temporal existence allowed him to embrace his fascination with prayer. "It was through language that I discovered prayer. It was through poetry that I rediscovered prayer. I didn't stop writing poems. I didn't stop creating. I didn't stop singing. I just sang in a different direction."

There was a need for priests within the Augustinian order, so after a year at Marylake, Di Cicco began theological studies at the University of Toronto. He drove down from the monastery every day to attend classes at St. Michael's and St. Basil's colleges. In his fourth year of studies, young directors at Marylake began replacing some of the orthodox religious traditions that he loved with more liberal and contemporary practices, so he transferred to the Archdiocese of Toronto. He was ordained to the priesthood in 1993, and began ministering to the largely Italian-speaking parishes in nearby Woodbridge and Mississauga.

Today, Di Cicco balances his liturgical duties with professional and poet laureate obligations. He delivers Sunday sermons at parishes throughout Etobicoke although, when needed, he performs other sacraments: confessions, baptisms, marriages. "Part of why I became a priest was to help people finish the poem of their lives and to help write it with them or they write mine," he says. "Because the poem on the page wasn't enough. I wanted the poem on the page and the poem of life to be interconnected."

At the age of fifty, Di Cicco ran into Denis De Klerck, the publisher of Mansfield Press, who persuaded him there was a generation who wanted his poetry back in circulation. Di Cicco produced *Living in Paradise* (2001), a series of new and collected poems. The collection captures the contours of his poetic journey – and life journey. Throughout his books there is often a continuous struggle to bridge the chasms – whether it is between art and science, the Italian culture of his childhood and the culture of North America, or the intellect and emotion. Indeed, the idea of being caught between two worlds is often a topic that governs their conversations, says his friend Robert Nusca. "You find that idea in biblical writings. Certainly it's behind St. Augustine's *City of God* – the two cities: the city of the world and the city of God, and how people feel themselves caught between these two realities."

Just as Di Cicco struggles for the incorporation of artistry and citizenry into daily life, he struggles for fusion within his poetry. "Poetry seeks a completion or homecoming ... I'm always getting at something – I think it's metaphysical. And metaphysical does not mean non-physical, it means something like heaven and earth coming together, something about disparities merging, something about how the divine is in the earthly, and how the earthly reflects the divine. Something about marrying things. I have this zeal and zest for things to be married."

Back outside the Italian Studies Department, Di Cicco is on another break. He lights another Matinee, and reminisces about a time a few years earlier when he travelled to Arizona along Highway 60, using a *National Geographic* map that a friend had given him. The map was drawn in 1942. Di Cicco got lost. ("Who would have thought the roads in a desert would have changed?" he charges.) With a little help from a gas-station attendant and a new map, Di Cicco found his way through the desert's silence.

He speaks about how much he loves to travel through deserts: the meditative nature inherent in their landscape; the solitude; the chance for reflection. But then he mentions how much he likes the bright neon cities that often surround them. And yet: the contrast between garish, corporeal cities of Reno and Vegas and the spiritual, almost godly, desert landscape is so glaring. But yes, of course: This would be the marriage of two worlds. This would be the marriage of heaven and earth.

Let Us Compare Anthologies

Harmonizing the Founding African-Canadian and Italian-Canadian Literary Collections[1]

For Ricardo Scipio[2]

GEORGE ELLIOTT CLARKE

If this essay is a tapestry, it is one threaded with the flamboyant gilt of *mea culpa* and *caveat lector*. Ignorant of the subtle, delicate, and intricate lineaments of Italian-Canadian literature and culture, I am foolhardy in hazarding any opinions about the ways in which the first anthology of Italian-Canadian literature, *Roman Candles: An Anthology of Poems by Seventeen Italo-Canadian Poets* (1978), edited by Pier Giorgio Di Cicco, may be alleged to share certain affinities with the first widely circulated African-Canadian literary anthology in English, *Canada In Us Now: The First Anthology of Black Poetry and Prose in Canada* (1976,)[3] edited by Harold Head. However, while I cannot legislate the history, politics, and institutions of Italian-

Canadian literature, I may acknowledge its apparent similarities with its African-Canadian counterpart, for their foundational anthologies address equivalent issues. The comparison is neither illicit nor illogical, for, despite their contrasting temporal, cultural, and linguistic origins, both of these minority-group-fostered Canadian literatures first achieved "critical mass" in the 1970s. Moreover, their mutual "coming-to-voice," so to speak, coincided with increased immigration from homelands and the announcement, by the Canadian state, on October 8, 1971, of an official policy to promote the development of a multicultural society within the superstructure of official bilingualism. Indeed, in its response to the report of the Royal Commission on Bilingualism and Biculturalism in 1971, the twenty-eighth Parliament of Canada, led by Liberal Prime Minister Pierre Elliott Trudeau, forecast the basic social environment in which the Head and Di Cicco anthologies would appear:

> Canadian identity will not be undermined by multi-culturalism. Indeed we believe that cultural pluralism is the very essence of Canadian identity ... To say that we have two official languages is not to say we have two official cultures, and no particular culture is more "official" than another. Multiculturalism is for all Canadians. (Qtd. in Tepper 197-8)

Too, both Di Cicco and Head – and their various contributors – had similar social agendas: 1) to articulate a group identity; 2) to reject both segregation and assimilation; 3) to create a dialogue with other "ethnic" Canadians. Consequently, Di Cicco's *Roman Candles* and its predecessor, Head's *Canada In Us Now*, advance their sociopolitical interests in complementary ways. This accidental, near-coalition offers an implicit defence of bureaucratized Multiculturalism,[4] while also underscoring the unity-within-diversity of distinct, but parallel, literary cultures.

Crucially, both *Roman Candles* and *Canada In Us Now* appeared in the wake of the promulgation of a federal Multiculturalism policy. Prompted by concerns for national unity, the program sought to improve Canadian national identity by promoting, said Prime Minister Trudeau, "confidence in one's own identity; out of this can grow respect for others and a willingness to share ideas, attitudes and assumptions" (qtd. in Tepper 197). Trudeau believed that "a vigorous policy of multiculturalism will help create this initial confidence. It can form the basis of a society which is based on fair play for all" (qtd. in Tepper 197). Though Trudeau's rhetoric is lacklustre and vague, the policy itself was revolutionary. York University history professor Irving Abella confirms that "Multiculturalism is innovative; it has enhanced our self-image; it has proven a life-saver to many communities; it has created pride where there had once only been pain; comfort where there was once only contempt..." (72). For Abella, Multiculturalism "came into being in order to open minds that for too long had been closed" and "to right a terrible historical wrong and to write [minorities] back into Canadian history" (78). For Hedy Fry, a former Secretary of State for Multiculturalism (1996-2000), the program is "the polar opposite of apartheid" (36). According to Emilio S. Binavince, a constitutional lawyer, Multiculturalism makes it possible for Canadian minorities to pursue "equal access to government power and the institutions of government" (91). Its supporters understand that Multiculturalism extends, to non-Anglo-Saxon and non-Gallic Canadian citizens, official recognition of their existence as minority groups within the state. This recognition was radical, for it detracted from the prevailing view of Canada as a white Franco-British state, where only Canadians of these heritages, espousing Protestant and Catholic versions of Christianity, could be considered complete citizens. Through official Bilingualism (established in 1969), the federal state argued that it was now responsive to Francophone (as well as Anglophone) Cana-

dians; through Multiculturalism, it now por-
trayed itself as representing all Canadians,
without distinguishing among different heritages. Whatever the "radical" implications of
this re-positioning of the Canadian state, federal
Liberal politicians were quick to attempt to reap
the usual electoral benefits.

By 1976 and 1978 then, when the Head and
Di Cicco anthologies appear, song-and-dance
multicultural festivals and celebrations were
commonplace.[5] True: Di Cicco's anthology was
funded by The Canada Council arts funding
agency [9] and Head's was published by the
Marxism-infused, New Canada Press. Neither
book received funding from the Multiculturalism Secretariat. Nevertheless, both entered an
environment where state Multiculturalism was
being instrumentalized as an opportunistic
means of cementing "ethnic" allegiances to the
governing Liberals, while also serving as a prop-
aganda bulwark against the independence-
minded, Quebec provincial government.[6] In
other words, while eschewing any imbrication
with state Multiculturalism in the 1970s, both
Head and Di Cicco produced works engaging
inevitably with its principal discourses: pro-
immigration, pro-"Canadian" identity, pro-
diversity, and pro-national unity (or anti-sepa-
ratism). Such an engagement was inevitable

because Multiculturalism seemed en-route, in the 1970s, to forging Canada into a "truly global and metropolitan community" (Kinsella 54) or "a multi-ethnic mosaic within which multiple allegiances are fostered" (Stanford 177). Head and Di Cicco participate in a discussion then that was heralding what Fo Niemi calls the "age of 'mosaic democracies'" (172). However, neither editor could articulate, in 1976 or 1978, a truly catholic multiculturalism, for both were pursuing, in occasionally clashing terms, culturally (ethnic) nationalist aesthetics and agendas.

In "We have come," his introduction to *Canada In Us Now*, Head, in fealty to the black liberation ethos then-popular among black intellectuals in urban Canada, voices an *ars poetica* of black power: "This anthology is representative of the collective consciousness of people in the act of liberating themselves (and us) from a legacy which denied their humanity and heaped scorn on the culture of colonial peoples" (7).[7] For Head, a South African native, the writers canvassed in his anthology "reaffirm the spirit of all mankind striving to be free" (7). Thus, he disparages "petty" work mandating "simply the pretty arrangement of words for the edification of a 'cultured' minority" (9). Head's dismissal of supposedly dismally bourgeois art dovetails with his publisher's sworn interest in publishing

126

"books and pamphlets that will be of assistance to the Canadian People's struggle for national liberation" [4]. Head's guiding principles are both Marxist and Pan-Africanist, representing an alliance between Anglo-Canadian nationalists anxious about US influence in Canada and black community activists anxious for greater influence within Canadian society.

In his preface, Di Cicco is briefer than Head and less directly "political." His impetus for assembling *Roman Candles* is purely cultural, not socialist. Feeling "isolated" from other Italian-Canadian writers, as well as self-conscious about his dual culture and heritage, he wants to found a conversation. Di Cicco offers no palaver of "liberation," no gestures toward a "collective consciousness." Instead, he organizes a conference of poets, more-or-less, who express a "bicultural sensibility" [9] – Italian and Anglo-Canadian.

Another difference also separates the two anthologists. Introducing his anthology, Head centralizes the black immigrant experience. The politics of dislocation and relocation are his writers' focus:

> The majority of the contributors to this anthology are new Canadians. Some have been here only four years, two have lived here for the past twenty years and three are fourth generation Canadians. (10)

127

Di Cicco applies an opposing emphasis:

> All the poets included have one sure thing in common – they are not emigrants. They were brought here by their families at an early age, and three were born in North America. [9]

Head feels that his set of mainly immigrant authors has made a political choice to realize black world liberation, in concert with Canadian aspirations to achieve a socialist society. Di Cicco classes his authors, in contrast, as practically native North Americans or Canadians; their usage of English cancels, Di Cicco believes, their putatively alien origins.

Indeed, unlike Head, Di Cicco claims an explicit Canadian identity for his contributors. By denying émigré status to children, Di Cicco suggests they are Canadian by birth. Yet, the authors' bios discredit this assumption. For instance, John Melfi, born in Italy in 1947, arrived in Canada in 1956; Joseph Ranallo, born in Italy in 1940, landed in Canada in 1952; Filippo Salvatore, born in Italy in 1948, was sixteen when his family removed to Canada (Biographical Notes 84-85).[8] The idea of a common "North America" [9] shared by Italian immigrants enables Di Cicco to count the U.S.-born Mike Zizis as Canadian (Biographical Notes 85).

Thus, the editor defines, strategically, his "Italo-Canadian" writers as Canadian.[9]

The contrasting emphases of Head and Di Cicco are underscored by Di Cicco's seeming riposte to Head's title, *Canada in Us Now: The First Anthology of Black Poetry and Prose in Canada*: "I decided to limit the work to that written in English, largely to avoid an anthology the title of which would be *The Italian Poets Writing in Canada*..." [9]. Di Cicco wishes to explore "what, if anything, these poets could bring to Anglo-Canadian poetry" [9], to accent their "fortunate and tragic position of having to live with two cultures, one more exterior than the other" [9-10]. Di Cicco's "Italo-Canadian" poets interest him for the ways in which they manifest Italianness within the dominant discourse of English, or, specifically, Anglo-Canadian literature.

For his part, Head ignores Canadian literature. The potential existence and availability of a dual "Black" and "Canadian" sensibility is irrelevant. His desire is to unify "blacks," those who happen to be "in Canada," not to promote integration with Canadians – who are pictured, implicitly, as white. Yes, Head recognizes that his contributors share with Anglo-Canadians a British heritage. They "were schooled in Shakespeare, Wordsworth, Blake, Byron, Shelley,

Keats, and Browning" and are from "Guyana, Trinidad, Barbados, St. Vincent, South Africa, Nigeria and Canada – all former British colonies" [7]. Still, Head's poets and prose writers hail from, fundamentally, "the Black World" (9), and their compositions "return, in spirit, to origins, to Africa where the work of the artist is even today at one with his [sic] community..." (8).

While Di Cicco seeks to identify the Italo-Canadian "displaced sensibility" [9] or "bicultural sensibility" [9] and its contribution – realized or potential – to English-Canadian poetry, Head is obsessed, strikingly, with how his authors replicate "Africa" in their subjects and rhetoric, for they belong to "the Third World" (10) – a purportedly primary allegiance. Head's writers are, he believes, building a Pan-Africanist, not a Canadian, literature. He sees, then, only the possibility of a "Black" and "Canadian" – i.e. white workers – liberation movement uniting to oppose American and European imperialist capitalism (11-12). There are "Blacks" and there are "Canadians" – no hyphenation necessary. The only 'hyphenated' Canadians[10] Head discusses, the so-called "Afro-Canadian" (10) – or multi-generational African-Canadian – people are flawed: they bear the stigma of "historical and psychological castra-

130

tion" (10).[11] Their "bicultural sensibility" – as Di Cicco would term it – is, here, a terrible liability. In sum, in his anthology preface, Head craves a unified black collectivity, within Canada, whose writings participate in a global, Pan-African, black empowerment movement, but whose politics leave room for opportune, leftist alliances with white Canadians: "You share our colonial heritage; your (our) liberation is not yet done. Your future lies with us every bit as much as our present lies with you" (12). Turning to Di Cicco, one notes that he disparages "Canadianism" [9], that is, Anglo-Canadian nationalism, to foreground "Italo-Canadian experience" [9] – that is, writers who "belong and do not belong" (10). Although Di Cicco rejects the Canuck nationalism Head supports, tacitly (to offset British and American nationalism), Di Cicco's emphasis on the dual cultural status of his writers is as contradictory as Head's description of black immigrants as "new Canadians" [10] who are, nevertheless, scribes of a black "Socialist International". Even though Head and Di Cicco strike contrasting attitudes toward Canada and immigrant populations, both oppose any model of monocultural white / "Anglo" Canadianness. Head expresses his dissent by collapsing Canadian identity into Pan-Africanism. Therefore, he writes that, following a "yesterday" when "we

131

were separated from Africa into Jamaica, Barbados, Trinidad, Guyana; Mandingo from Ashanti; Ashanti from Benin..."; and when "Canadians could count on one hand the black faces around Bathurst and Bloor Streets in Toronto," we will "tomorrow... be marching down the streets of Pretoria on our way to celebrate life in Soweto." (11) African-Canadians are imagined as displaced and divided Africans who will re-unite in the triumphant celebration of a liberated Africa. This vision is pseudo-Garveyite. Likewise Di Cicco resents "the sheer force of Canadianism" [9], that is to say, Anglo-Canadian cultural nationalism, which stifles "Italo-Canadian" expression. He prefers writers who will remake English- (and French-) Canadian literature and culture in a new, Italian-Canadian image.

Despite their like tactical challenges to a Canadian "culture" dominated by, says Head, whites, and, says Di Cicco, Anglos, the editors differ on strategy. Head considers blacks who happen now to live in Canada; Di Cicco is concerned with Italian-Canadians who feel stranded between an Italy where they are not remembered and a Canada that (super)imposes an Anglo (or Franco) culture upon their own. Head views Canada implicitly as a "white" country that is a nearly irrelevant host for a black/African population in provisional exile. For Di Cicco, the Italian immigrant quarrel with English (and French) Canada is a battle among Europeans-in-exile, with "Italians" protesting the tendency of Anglo-Saxons and Gauls to hog Canada for themselves. In other words, Head constructs, from "Black" Canada, a Pan-African Union established within the blank, waste space of semi-colonial Canada; Di Cicco seeks, in contrast, a *concordat* with English-Canadian culture and literature.

Despite their clashing, philosophical "anthems", Head and Di Cicco compose anthologies that harmonize remarkably. Both editors include seventeen poets. (Head also enlists three fiction writers.) Head's "crew" hails from all corners of the African Diaspora, but also number a "Coloured" South African and two Caribbean-born, South Asians, all assembled under the rubric "Black," a *sign* protean and cosmopolitan here. Di Cicco selects writers from Italy, Canada, and the United States. However, his approach also approximates multiculturalism, for the writers from these three locales matured in vastly different societies. Head "imports" the "black world" to Canada; Di Cicco introduces Canadians to a multifarious, "Italian" identity and experience.[12]

Di Cicco closes his Preface with a poem, "My Genealogy," by John Robert Colombo, that speaks to a family lineage of incessant cultural

fusion and transfusion. Its last four stanzas merit
recitation here:

9.

Blood flows through my veins
at different speeds:
Greek, French-Canadian.
Sometimes it mixes.

10.

At times I feel close
to the Aegean,
the Cote d'Azure,
the Lombard Plain,
and the Black Forest.

11.

I seldom feel close
to the Rocky Mountains,
the Prairies,
the Great Lakes,
or the cold St. Lawrence.
What am I doing in Toronto?

12.

If this means being Canadian,
I am a Canadian. (11-12)

Di Cicco sounds Colombo so as to flesh out his
own precept, "that the true [Canadian] citizen
remains a foreigner if only to remain a citizen of

the world" (10). Head backs a similar internationalism; his Caribbean-born contributors are, he feels, "a new adjunct to the Black and Canadian communities" (11), and that all blacks "offer other Canadians a unique opportunity – a window – and a tangible link – with the Third World" (11). Head urges, to recast Di Cicco, that "the true Black Canadian remains a foreigner if only to remain a citizen of the larger black world."

The poem that best articulates Head's aims in *Canada In Us Now* is Liz Cromwell's "We have come," whose title also brands Head's introduction. Here is its opening stanza:

To Toronto we have come as men
Seeking shapes in a long lost dream
Across the green seas.
We who dried our blackness in the sun
Have come as bondsmen without shame or home
To seek a loaf of fame, redeem our pride
Imbibe the juice of pain
To do what we as creatures of past dreams
Of smoke have made us. (60)

These "bondsmen" of Cromwell – and Head – face a major peril: to forget their original, Caribbean heritages and thus become "whitewashed Negroes/ of the much-touted sad mosaic" – of multiculturalism (60). To avoid this danger, Head's anthology seeks to reconstitute a coherent black community within the forbidding, "white" vastness of Canada. Similarly, Di Cicco wishes to save "Italo-Canadians" from the "isolationism" created by Anglo-Canadian nationalism [9] as well as from "the convenience of a melting-pot" – or assimilationism (10). Thus, he engineers an anthology. Italian-Canadian scholar Joseph Pivato recognizes the importance of such cultural work:

> The publication of ethnic anthologies... creates an identity for the group or generation... stimulates reader interest in the writers as a group... encourages the writers to publish their own work... begins to create critical and academic interest in the writers. Pier Giorgio Di Cicco's 1978 anthology of Italian-Canadian poets, *Roman Candles*, did all of these things and more... (67)

To revise Head, then, Di Cicco sallies against a future of utterly Gallicized or Saxonized Italians.

Crucially, both Head and Di Cicco defend the maintenance of distinctive, cultural heritages in an officially Multicultural society. By pursuing a definite policy of "hyphenated Canadianism," a concept verified in his use of the term "Italo-Canadian," Di Cicco rejects the rightist liberal view that "the 'hyphenated' concept can undermine Canadian identity" (Cardozo & Musto 9). By showcasing poets who voice a "bicultural

136

sensibility" [9], Di Cicco flouts such critics as U.S. liberal, Arthur Schlesinger, Jr., who deems multiculturalism "dangerously divisive. It encourages government to segregate citizens along racial, ethnic, and linguistic fault-lines" (qtd. in Jan Brown 68). Di Cicco's practice also counters the vision of Japanese-Canadian cultural activist R.L. Gabrielle Nishiguchi, who alleges the hyphen is "that tiny splash of ink uniting words but distancing worlds" (112). By compiling *Roman Candles*, Di Cicco offers an eloquent riposte to those who, in the name of advancing Canadian (or Quebecois) unity, request the erasure of minority cultural specificity.[13]

Although Head rues the only "hyphenated" Canadian group he discusses, i.e. the "Afro-Canadian" (10); he does not rue multiculturalism. His chief passion is the unification of intellectual black and "Third World" émigrés and exiles here. His totalizing interpretation of "Black" nixes a hyphen. The rhetoric of black consciousness and anti-imperialism is *the* rallying point for black – and brown (Asian) – intellectuals displaced in(to) Canada. From this perspective, *Canada in Us Now* is an inversion of its more "natural" title: "Us In Canada Now." Certainly, Head's interest is not Canadian citizenship, but the raising of a phalanx of African-heritage intellectuals to continue to agitate, from a "Canadian" vantage point, for anti-racism in Canada and anti-apartheid and anti-colonialism abroad.

Di Cicco accents the "bicultural," Italo-Canadian identity of his writers, but his anthology affirms multiculturalism by appearing in English. But the apparent influence of Jewish-Canadian writers upon at least three of the *Roman Candle* poets presents another glimpse of multiculturalism at work (or play). Di Cicco dedicates a poem to Tom Wayman ("The Poem Becomes Canadian" 38). Filippo Salvatore's poem, "Three Poems for Giovanni Caboto" (1978), replicates the spirit of an Irving Layton poem addressing the statues of Hebrew prophets in a Quebecois, Catholic cathedral, "On Seeing the Statuettes of Ezekiel and Jeremiah in the Church of Notre Dame" (1956). Like Layton, Salvatore features a speaker who comments ironically on the appropriation of a great, ancestral compatriot by an alien culture. His persona engages in a monologue addressing a statue of so-called John Cabot, the Italian explorer who claimed the "New World" for Britain:

> Giovanni, they erected you a monument,
> but they changed your name; here
> they call you John. And you
> look at them from your stony
> pedestal with a hardly perceivable
> grin on your bronze lips. (14)

Layton's persona sounds much like Salvatore's speaker:

> They have given you French names
> and made you captive, my rugged
> troublesome compatriots;
> your splendid beards, here, are epicene,
> plaster white
> and your angers
> unclothed with Palestinian hills quite lost
> in this immense and ugly edifice. (19)

Len Gasparini's poem, "The Photograph of My Grandfather Reading Dante" (1967), echoes A.M. Klein's lyric, "Heirloom" (1940). In the case of both poets, the speaker bonds with a patriarch by recalling, wistfully, the latter's dedication to text – poetic or scriptural. Klein's poem forges the connection between paternal ancestry and literal, cultural literacy with nostalgic, Romantic rhetoric:

> My father bequeathed me no wide estates;
> No keys and ledgers were my heritage;
> Only some holy books with yahrzeit dates
> Writ mournfully upon a blank front page –
> Books of the Baal Shem Tov, and of his wonders;
> Pamphlets upon the devil and his crew;
> Prayers against road demons, witches, thunders;
> And sundry other tomes for a good Jew [...]
> These are my coat of arms, and these unfold
> My noble lineage, my proud ancestry!(157-8)

Gasparini's lyric memorializes a two-genera-
tions-back, paternal reader:

> Every evening
> he would sit for hours
> in his favorite old rocking chair,
> holding a glass of homemade wine,
> with the *Divina Commedia* in his lap
> and a snuff box on the table beside him.
>
> Under a plain parchment lampshade
> that haloed his venerable head,
> my mother's father, Luigi, would
> immerse himself in profundities.
>
> And while the rest of our family played
> cards or listened to Italian music,
> I would study his wrinkled, serene
> face and love him... (28)

Like Klein, Gasparini delineates his literary
paternity by appealing to the example of a studious male forebear. For Klein, it is the father
who reads Hebrew scripture and its glosses; for
Gasparini, it is the grandfather who reads Dante.
The parallels between both poets' poems do not
end here. Klein's father, in his reading, left
"snuff... on this page, now brown and old"
(158). Gasparini's grandfather sits reading with
"a snuff box on the table beside him" (28). One
more intertextual linkage is Gasparini's use of
the rocking chair; this reference points the

reader to Klein's most popular book of poems, *The Rocking Chair and Other Poems* (1948). These allusive connections suggest an Italian-Canadian interest in the Jewish-Canadian success in building a new culture in an alien land, while eschewing both isolation and assimilation.

Canada in Us Now shows no interest in any Canada-located, minority group save African-heritage people. Instead, Head's writers display a multicultural vision by limning a Pan-African and Third World-oriented blackness. The anthology scribes, describes, and prescribes a polyphonous, international, and kaleidoscopic blackness, the very form of "African-Canadianité."[14] Thus, poet Vibert Cambridge anatomizes contemporary West Indian immigration as a further globalization of the African Diaspora:

> You may have seen him in Panama's Canal....
> England's
> Brixton, Balham,
> Birmingham and Bradford,
> Guyana's Tiger Bay,
> Trinidad's La Basse,
> Jamaica's Dungle
> And America's Bedford Stuyvesant.
> You can now see
> him in Canada's [i.e. Toronto's] Bathurst
> and occasionally
> Brampton and Bramalea. (24)

Head's poem, "Resumé," rewrites a job-application form to present an archetypal black leftist whose "Past Employment" saw him participate in the liberation of Algeria, The Congo, Kenya, Cuba, and Vietnam (84), while his "Position Desired" is "Restoration of dignity/ & respect to the Indian nations/ bantustand [sic] in Babylon" (84). The itinerant, South African exile, Arthur Nortje, in the course of his immigration to Canada, complains that "Bitter costs exorbitantly at London/ airport"; critiques "the bull-dozer civilization/ of Fraser and Mackenzie" in British Columbia; recalls "the blond aura of the past/ at Durban or Johannesburg" in South Africa; and applies the *ubi sunt* rhetorical formula to native South Africans: "Where are the mineworkers, the compound Africans,/ your Zulu ancestors, where are/ the root-eating, bead-charmed Bushmen, the Hottentot sufferers?" (112-113). His own exile and emigration becomes emblematic of the original displacement of South Africa's native population. In *Canada in Us Now*, then, multiculturalism is championed, not by stressing congruencies between the writings and experiences of blacks and other Canadian minorities, but by marking the pluralism of "Black Canada" and its *de facto* linkages – cultural and political – to other peoples of colour. Therefore, Head includes two Indo-Caribbean writers (Darryl Dean and

142

Harold Sonny Ladoo) as well as one Caribbean Aboriginal (Arawak) writer (David Campbell).

Reflecting its thematic, "bicultural sensibility," *Roman Candles'* contributors discuss Canada-located crises which debut in the loss of language or culture and which climax with the death of an elder. In "The Man Called Beppino," then, Di Cicco tells of a man, perhaps his own father, who, as a barber in Baltimore, Maryland, "works for nothing, because his english [sic]/ is less than fine; the customers like him,/ and the man is easily duped, he believes in the/ honest dollar, and is offered peanuts in return" (31). Antonino Mazza, in his poem, "Canadese," commands other Italian-Canadians to remember their heritage: "Don't try to reject your mother tongue,/ in our cage, it is wrong;/ do canaries smother their private song?" (39). His poem, "Death in Italy" recounts the macabre surrealism of mourning, in Canada, the death of a father in Italy:

> Ah, not to have seen one's father die!
> ...Mute days followed. Heartsunk
> we stayed at home in one grave lit room
> my mother's dress turned black, the men wore death
> for ties, black arm bands and other sorrow signs
> and bands of friends appeared
> to pay their last respects in absentia.
> They are ghostly people with ghastly voices
> when they relate their own Death in Italy stories.
> (40)

The special pain of separation from parents and relatives "abandoned" to the "Old Country" is a common thematic. Thus, Tony Pignataro states succinctly, "Life was a long distance telephone call / across the Atlantic" (49). Mary di Michele writes about a Canadian-raised daughter visiting the Italian village of her childhood, then dialing "home", ironically, to Canada: "Pronto, I hear my mother cough,/ across the Atlantic" (60). "Enigmatico" portrays di Michele's heritage of ocean-wide estrangement: "she cries out caught/ with one bare foot in a village in the Abruzzi,/ the other busy with cramped English speaking toes in Toronto,/ she strides the Atlantic legs spread/ like a colossus" (62).

Di Cicco's poets straddle Italy and Canada – or, at least they attempt to bridge both countries. But Head's poets still seek a homeland that is fully their own – a Canada that is welcoming, or a Caribbean that is truly free of neo-colonial control. Vibert Cambridge states, "We have until tomorrow to make our countries/ our countries," and asks, "When will we stop making our countries / their countries?/ And still have no country to call our own?" ("Historical" 29). In her piece, "The raping of the womb," Felizze Mortune imagines a black birth as the instantiation of an assumption of war: "i stuck out my

144

black skull/ through mother's vagina/ my first
reaction to the real world/ was a cry of revolt"
(102). No black person, whether born in Canada
or not, can evade the historical mission of revolt.
Head presents a similar sentiment:

In Babylon
When a woman gives birth
Do not ask if it is a boy or girl
We are soldiers
The moment we are born. ("In Babylon" 85)

One does not need to know the Rastafarian concept of "Babylon" to understand that it applies
to the capitalist, secularist, and "white" Occi-
dent – including Canada. In his introduction,
Head may call for an alliance between Canadians and "Blacks," but, here, he is clear that
Canada is so problematically ensconced within
the Euro-American, capital-imperial nexus that,
here, too, black children born within its borders
are fated to be fighters – or liberators, guerillas.
If Di Cicco's Italian-Canadian poets approach
multiculturalism via their biculturality, Head's
"African" assembly must foreground a heritage
of (racial) struggle that links all black people,
that is to say, they must vaunt a *black* multiculturalism. Indeed, the anthology is "dedicated to
the spirit and ideals of the Second World Black

and African Festival of Arts and Culture to be held in Nigeria in 1977" [2].

Introducing *The Anthology of Italian-Canadian Writing* (1998), editor Joseph Pivato recognizes that, prior to the arrival of Di Cicco's anthology, "There were many Italian writers and many books by Italians living in Canada, but they did not constitute a conscious literature" (Introduction 11). At this point, their writing represented "individual works produced by isolated writers who did not see themselves as creators of a new literature but as Italian writers in exile, or travellers or as writers in Canada who adopted the new language" (Introduction 11). Head's 1976 anthology features a like psychology: the "Us in Canada Now" are not yet African-Canadian, nor is their writing consciously that of Black Canadians, but rather, it is representative of "Black Poetry and Prose *in* Canada" as the subtitle says (cover, my italics). Or, as the dedication puts it, the anthology presents "the collective consciousness of the African diaspora in Canada today" [2]. Nevertheless, Head, too, like Di Cicco for Italian-Canadian writing, helps to usher in African-Canadian literature by consciously grouping together writers of disparate cultural and national origins. While neither Head nor Di Cicco engages with official Multiculturalism, their respective groupings of

"Blacks in Canada" and "Italo-Canadians" could only make sense in the context of a society dominated racially by whites and culturally by Anglos and Francos. In other words, their respective writer-collages – Pan-African/Canadian and Trans-Atlantic/ Mediterranean/Canadian – conjured up an intra-communal multiculturalism that made official Multiculturalism less stable, that is to say, more dynamic, whatever its status quo proclivities.

Notes

1. This essay was sculpted for two presentations: the Keynote Address for the Association for Italian Canadian Writers, Toronto, Ontario, on May 27, 2002; and for the "Canada: Model for a Multicultural State" Conference, Edmonton, Alberta, on September 27, 2002.
2. Ricardo Scipio is an Afro-Trinidad-born photographer based in Vancouver, B.C. His Latinate names are as much a result of slavery as are my Anglo-Celtic ones.
3. Head's anthology, as I have pointed out in previous scholarship, is actually the *third* African-Canadian anthology. However, it was the first one to attempt to canvass black writing from across Canada. It was preceded by *Black Chat: An Anthology of Black Poets* (1973), edited by Camille Haynes, and *One Out of Many: A Collection of Writings by 21 Black Women in Ontario* (1975), edited by Liz Cromwell.
4. When capitalized, "Multiculturalism" refers to the official, federal Government policy and programme; when it is not capitalized, "multiculturalism" refers to the general concept.
5. The Liberal government of Trudeau may have sought to use multiculturalism to secure the electoral allegiances of "ethnic" communities in the largest Canadian cities, as well as to bolster "national unity," in the wake of the election of the pro-Québec-independence Parti Québécois, in Quebec, in 1976. Yet, such Machiavellian manoeuvring is common-place in governing. In their essay on Canadian multiculturalism, Andrew Cardozo and Louis Musto affirm "politics is the stuff of most government policies" (8). One critic of Multi-

culturalism as state policy, then-Independent Member of Parliament Jan Brown, argued, in 1996, that Canadians find the concept confusing because it "can encompass folk songs, dance, food, festivals, arts and crafts, museums, heritage languages, ethnic studies, ethnic presses, race relations, culture sharing, and human rights" (65).

6. In 1996, Bloc Québécois Member of Parliament Christiane Gagnon wagered that the establishing of Multiculturalism was a federal reaction to the "expression of Quebec's desire for independence, coming as it did shortly after the October crisis [of 1970]..." (43). From this nationalist Québécois perspective, Multiculturalism promotes "cultural differences" at the expense of "the concept of integration that would recognize the rights of members of ethnic groups and their equal participation in society" (43). Most destructively, "the whole dialectic of two founding peoples [the formation of Canada as a compact between British and French peoples] with their own language and culture was submerged and diluted in this ocean of other languages and cultures" (43). This critique of Multiculturalism has prospered for, as Fo Niemi reported in 1996, "Since the adoption of multiculturalism in 1971, there has been only one French-speaking minister capable of communicating with and clarifying multiculturalism among seven million French-speaking Canadians who are generally mistrustful of this policy" (168). Presumably, Niemi was referring to then-Heritage Canada Minister Sheila Copps (1993-2003), who spoke French, English, and Italian, a linguistic profile shared by her eventual successor, Liza Frulla (2004-6).

7. Ironically, though, such rhetoric was already a spent force in 1976. While the African-American "Black Power" and "Black Arts" movements flourished from 1965 to 1975, their echoes in Canada arrived later (in 1968 – see the Black Writers Conference in Montreal) and ended later (in 1978 – see the penultimate demise of the National Black Coalition of Canada), but were never as revolutionary as their US originators. The reasons for the lower intensity of these movements in Canada were: 1) a relatively smaller black population residing in disconnected pockets across the world's second-largest country; 2) the variegated cultural allegiances of so-called blacks; and 3) the primacy of linguistic issues and state-nationalist politics over "race" (save for First Nations peoples).

8. One must wonder about the reasons for Di Cicco's intellectual violence in his wiping away of the Italian childhoods of his writers.

9. Certainly, Head also "Canadianizes" his writers, classifying all of them as "Canadian" – "new" and otherwise (10). However, their blackness is more important than their Canadian citizenship.

10. The rhetoric about "hyphenated" identities in Canada hearkens back

148

to Progressive Conservative Prime Minister John George Diefen-
baker (1957-1963), whose nationalism insisted on a singular Canadian identity: "One Canada, one nation, my Canada, your Canada,
cannot be a hyphenated Canada" (qtd. in Nishiguchi 111). Diefen-
baker himself seems to have imported this sentiment from U.S. Pres-
ident Theodore Roosevelt (1901-1909), who warned against the
dangers of "hyphenated Americans" in a New York City speech in
October 1915, see Barnett 14. According to this liberal perspective,
whether Rooseveltian or Diefenbakerian, to be "hyphenated" – as in
"Japanese-Canadian" – is to be divided. In defence of the "hyphen,"
Italian-Canadian scholar Joseph Pivato argues that, given the history
of terms like "French-Canadian" in Canada, it is difficult to see how
other, generally smaller minorities could eschew the hyphenation of
their own identities (48). Pivato also notes, "Hyphenation in
Western Canada does not seem to carry the same negative connota-
tion as in Central Canada. It is common practice here to use terms
like: Ukrainian-Canadian, Chinese-Canadian, Hungarian-Canadian,
Haitian-Canadian, Italian-Canadian, and Polish-Canadian" (51 n.1).
A Chinese-Canadian commentator issues a strong defence of the
hyphen in her self-conception. Hear Lillian To: "Am I less Canadian
because I am a woman or because I am of Chinese origin? ... We
cannot all be Anglo-Saxon white males... Unless you produce clones
or go through a purge, you cannot eliminate hyphenated Canadians" (203).

11. Perhaps Head was influenced by the thought of Trinidadian-Cana-
dian playwright Lennox Brown, who declared, in 1972, "There is
no substantial Black culture in Canada" (8) and that "Black culture
in Canada was born in the cradle of Whiteness" (6).

12. Antonio D'Alfonso notes, "Italy is not a unity but a mosaic" (37).

13. Introducing *The Battle Over Multiculturalism* (1997), editors Cardozo and Musto defend the concept, recognizing that "Cultural
diversity existed in Canada well before the arrival of European set-
tlers. The Aboriginal and Inuit peoples were here first, and each
were composed of sub-groups with their own language, culture, and
social organization" (7). Pivato affirms that, with the appearance of
Roman Candles, its contributors (including himself) "answered the
call, discovered a group of writers, a receptive audience and we
never looked back" (35). In fact, "The literary phenomenon of
Italian-Canadian writing as a new body of writing was first recognized by Pier Giorgio Di Cicco in 1975-76 when he began to collect
poems for his, now famous, anthology..." (38). Introducing the
anthology, *Swallowing Clouds: An Anthology of Chinese-Canadian
Poetry* (1999), co-editor Andy Quan observes, "This anthology of
poetry comes from a place that is both real and mythical – a place

that exists concretely, and one that is created as we speak its name: *Chinese-Canada*" (7). Like Head and Di Cicco before him, he recognizes that the construction of an anthology announces the existence of a "new" and "multicultural" community:

...I had to see how diverse a people we [are]. Not only from Canton, immigrants came from all parts of China, from Taiwan, and from bustling Hong Kong. Perhaps they arrived in Canada by way of other continents, via Europe, Africa, Latin America, and Australia, or East Asian countries such as Malaysia, Singapore, Indonesia, and Vietnam... It is a diverse group such as this that can give meaning to a name. Chinese-Canada. And if the poets here are all to be grouped together in a Chinese-Canadian poetry anthology, then we are witnessing multiple creations. First of all, it is the creation of a community, a "we" rather than "I," a gathering of diverse people who presume a cultural coherence due to our "Chinese"-ness. Next, we see how this characteristic of race and culture attaches itself to a nation-state, the great snowy plains and water country – oh, Canada... (7)

Quan's discovery of a *multicultural* "Chinese-Canada," one created by its artists, also creates the grounds for an engagement with other multicultural communities in Canada. Thus, when Quan writes, "With our poems, we're also saying ... *We are here*," in Canada," he echoes not only Head's introduction, "We have come," but also a concluding phrase of my introduction to my edited anthology, *Eyeing the North Star: Directions in African-Canadian Literature* (1997): "And we are here. Where we have always been. Since 1605" (xxv).

14. See my article, "Contesting a Model Blackness," for a full discussion of these major aspects of African-Canadian identity.

Works Cited

Abella, Irving. "Multiculturalism, Jews, and the Forging of the Canadian Identity." In Cardozo & Musto. 71-89.

Barnett, Derek. "Ethnic branding." Letters to the Editor. *The Times*. [London] Wednesday, August 17, 2005. 14.

Binavince, Emilio S. "The Role of Ethnic Minorities in the Pursuit of Equality and Multiculturalism." In Cardozo and Musto. 90-100.

Brown, Jan. "Independent MP: Culture as an Individual Responsibility." In Cardozo and Musto. 60-8.

Brown, Lennox. "A Crisis: Black Culture in Canada." *Black Images.* 1.1 (January 1972): 4-8.

Cambridge, Vibert. "Historical Position No. 2." In *Canada in Us Now.* 28-9.

——. "The West Indian... a continuous position." In *Canada In Us Now.* 24-7.

Cardozo, Andrew, and Louis Musto, eds. *The Battle Over Multiculturalism: Does it help or hinder Canadian unity?* Volume 1. Ottawa: PSI Publishing, 1996.

——. "Introduction: identifying the Issues." In Cardozo and Musto. 7-15.

Clarke, George Elliott. "Contesting a Model Blackness: A Meditation on African-Canadian African Americanism, or The Structures of African Canadianité." *Odysseys Home: Mapping African-Canadian Literature.* Toronto: University of Toronto Press, 2002. 27-70.

——. Introduction. *Eyeing the North Star: Directions in African-Canadian Literature.* Ed. George Elliott Clarke. Toronto: McClelland & Stewart, 1997. xi-xxv.

Colombo, John Robert. "My Genealogy." In Di Cicco. 10-11.

Cromwell, Liz, ed. *One Out of Many: A Collection of Writings by 21 Black Women in Ontario.* Toronto: WACACRO Productions, 1975.

——. "We have come." In *Canada In Us Now.* 60.

D'Alfonso, Antonio. *In Italics: In Defense of Ethnicity.* Toronto: Guernica Editions, 1996.

Di Cicco, Pier Giorgio. Preface. In *Roman Candles.* 9-10.

——. "The Poem Becomes Canadian." In *Roman Candles.* 38.

——. "The Man Called Beppino." In *Roman Candles.* 31-2.

——. Ed. *Roman Candles: An Anthology of Poems by Seventeen Italo-Canadian Poets.* Toronto: Hounslow Press, 1978.

di Michele, Mary. "Across the Atlantic." In *Roman Candles.* 60.

——. "Enigmatico." In *Roman Candles.* 62.

Fry, Hedy. "Liberal Party: A Continued Commitment to the Ideals of Multiculturalism." In Cardozo and Musto. 35-41.

Gagnon, Christiane. "Bloc Québécois: Integration Rather Than Multiculturalism." In Cardozo and Musto. 42-5.

Gasparini, Len. "The Photograph of My Grandfather Reading Dante." In *Roman Candles.* 28.

Haynes, Camille, ed. *Black Chat: An Anthology of Black Poets.* Montreal: Black and Third World Students Association, Dawson College, 1973.

Head, Harold, ed. *Canada In Us Now: The First Anthology of Black Poetry and Prose in Canada.* Toronto: NC Canada Press, 1976.

——. "Resumé." In *Canada In Us Now.* 84.

——. "We have come." Introduction. In *Canada In Us Now.* 7-12.

Kinsella, Noël A. "Progressive Conservative Party: Guiding Our Future Through an Understanding of the Past." In Cardozo and Musto. 54-9.

Klein, A.M. "Heirloom." *The Collected Poems of A.M. Klein*. Ed. Miriam Waddington. Toronto: McGraw Hill-Ryerson, 1974.

———. *The Rocking Chair and Other Poems*. Toronto: The Ryerson Press, 1948.

Layton, Irving. "On Seeing the Statuettes of Ezekiel and Jeremiah in the Church of Notre Dame." *The Poems of Irving Layton*. Ed. Eli Mandel. Toronto: McClelland & Stewart, 1977. 19.

Mazza, Antonino. "Canadese." In *Roman Candles*. 39.

———. "Death in Italy." In *Roman Candles*. 40-1.

Mortune, Felizze. "The raping of the womb." In *Canada In Us Now*. 102.

Niemi, Fo. "Quebec, Canada and Multiculturalism: A Vision for the 21st Century." In Cardozo and Musto. 164-72.

Nishiguchi, R.L. Gabrielle. "True North Strong and Hyphen-Free." In Cardozo and Musto. 111-4.

Nortje, Arthur. "Immigrant." In *Canada In Us Now*. 112-3.

Pignataro, Tony. "The Immigrant." In *Roman Candles*. 48-9.

Pivato, Joseph. *Echo: Essays on Other Literatures*. Toronto: Guernica Editions, 1994.

———. Introduction. *The Anthology of Italian-Canadian Writing*. Ed. Joseph Pivato. Toronto: Guernica Editions, 1998. 9-17.

Quan, Andy. Introduction. *Swallowing Clouds: An Anthology of Chinese-Canadian Poetry*. Eds. Andy Quan and Jim Wong-Chu. Vancouver: Arsenal-Pulp Press, 1999. 7-10.

Salvatore, Filippo. "Three Poems for Giovanni Caboto." In *Roman Candles*. 13-6.

Stanford, C. Lloyd. "How to Advance National Unity: A Professional and Personal Perspective." In Cardozo and Musto. 173-82.

Tepper, Elliott L. "Multiculturalism as a Response to an Evolving Society." In Cardozo and Musto. 183-200.

To, Lilian. "A Must for B.C., a Must for Canada." In Cardozo and Musto. 201-6.

The Urban Poetry
of Pier Giorgio Di Cicco

In one of his first addresses as poet-laureate of
Toronto, Pier Giorgio Di Cicco observed that
"when literature deals with cities it not only
traces the human engagement with a city, it
measures a city's generosity to the human experience" ("Dynamics"). Indeed, the eclectic intersection of histories, cultures, and bodies in cities
have inspired a long literary tradition of poets
who were attracted to the visual spectacle of the
metropolis but also repulsed by its excesses – its
potential for alienation, violence, and human
misery. Writing at the beginning of the industrial
revolution, Wordsworth described the "din of
towns and cities" as "the still, sad music of humanity," ushering in the new reality of urban
industrialization with its factories, smoke stacks,
and faceless workers. A century later, T.S. Eliot
described London in a similar way, as an "unreal
city" which had "undone so many" under its
desolate "brown fog of a winter dawn." Di
Cicco also writes about London, describing its

famous tower as "that terrible armoury with crows on it," a place which, after the tourist crowds are gone, "resumes a serious death/ recovers something/ the purpose of itself, a color of ash/ containing its own logic, like screams" (*Circular Dark* 55). For Baudelaire, the city was a propitious space for the "man of the crowd" who ventured into the streets of nineteenth century Paris in order to experience the city and depict it in his modernist tableaus. If the visual spectacle of the city provided intrigue and inspiration for the flâneur, it also evoked scenes of shock and horror that was reflected in his poetry: "dans les plis sinueux des vieilles capitales, où tout, même l'horreur, tourne aux enchantements, je guette, obéissant à mes humeurs fatales, des êtres singuliers, décrépits et charmants." With the modernist aesthetic ushered in by Baudelaire, the city is both praised and reviled, but more importantly, it becomes a mirror of human subjectivity, as the urban landscape comes to reflect both the anguish and the ecstasy of the modernist urban dweller. Baudelaire's paradoxes in *Les Fleurs du Mal* are echoed in Di Cicco's *Dark Time of Angels*.

I would suggest that Di Cicco shares an affinity with these modernist precursors in that the city in his poetry is figured as a space of memory and desire, but also of alienation and loss. Always, it is a space interpreted through and reflective of the embodied sensibilities of the poet, be it in terms of the displaced sensibility of the ethnic subject at a loss to create a cohesive immigrant narrative, or in terms of the poet attempting to arrive at the transcendent by immersing himself in the immanent – the sensory stimuli of the city.

Di Cicco has been inspired by and situated in a variety of cities – Baltimore, Montreal, Toronto, but also the "mythic" Italian cities of his immigrant forebears – Arezzo, Rome, Venice. While each of these spaces evokes personal memory and family history, they also speak of the larger immigrant narrative that is too often reduced to an almost invisible trace upon the North-American landscape. This "dual perspective," which has been much discussed within the context of Italian-Canadian and other minority literatures (Pivato), re-creates the city as an unstable, dream-like landscape rife with intersecting and often contradictory images, spaces, linguistic codes, and histories. Elsewhere, I have discussed the spatialization of this dualistic identity wherein the dislocation of the "ethnic flâneur" (Beneventi, 216) manifests itself in literature through the metaphorical layering of the space of cultural origins (Italy), and the space of adoption (American or Canadian cities). These "heterotopic spaces," to borrow Foucault's term, conflate past and present, memory and fiction, in an attempt to re-situate or re-territorialize an ethnic subject coming to terms with the circumstances of history that have brought him or her to this place. This poetry of "radical dislocation," as Boelhower puts it, "is a geographical strategy that suggests an aesthetic of spatial juxtaposition" (231). Di Cicco engages in just such a strategy in his attempt to grasp the historical significations attached to particular spaces in the city; his narrators experience an embodied spatiality informed by the circumstances of personal and immigrant history, but also of its absences – the spectral selves that may have existed had migration never taken place.

Di Cicco spent many of his formative years in Baltimore, Maryland, and attributes to the urban landscape of this mid-sized American city the "double-consciousness" of the ethnic subject. It is figured as a space of memory and loss – of the linguistic and cultural signifiers of the *patria*, but, more importantly, the loss of his father who sat "under his mimosa by the highway, fifty pounds underweight" (*Tough Romance* 9). The juxtaposition of Italian and American spatial contexts is also evident in "Remembering Baltimore, Arezzo," where residents of the city are "perched on their solitudinous thrones wherever the heart has brought them," suggesting the absent father, but also many other immigrants like him whose dreams of an America paved with "streets of gold" have been tempered by the economic realities of class and ethnicity.

The "telescoping" of spaces in the immigrant imaginary reveals itself in Di Cicco's description of the family home, which is "not far from here, though you would think it many miles" (*Tough Romance* 8). This "chronotopic system" provides "not only a way of seeing but also a way of thinking," a "perspectival mechanism" which shows "how the ethnic subject proceeds in creating ethnic space within Canadian culture" (Boelhower 231). If the body of the father is absent, then that of the son is "the last outpost, a huge construct of blood," as he realizes that immigration has relegated his father to silence and to a grave in a strange city. The ghosts of the past "wash us down to Baltimore, out the Chesapeake, round the Atlantic, round the world" (*Tough Romance* 8). Here the "return journey" is symbolically undertaken in reverse, as the loss of the father instigates the son to return to the place of origin, to "a small town in the shade of a cypress, with nowhere to go but be still again" (*Tough Romance* 8). The city is here read as a metonym of loss, impotence, alienation, and death – trapping the immigrant in a cold embrace from which he will not emerge. The narrator's "originating ghosts" have become floating, disincarnated traces, as "the genealogical project, the politics of memory, the double perspectivism of the subject are all operating, and as ethnic he is both everywhere and nowhere" (Boelhower 242).

The image of the city as a lure or trap to immigrants is also articulated in "October Montreal," where the city is "damp and blue this month" and the world itself seems "evacuated" (*Tough Romance* 3). The cross atop Mount Royal which overlooks the city "bows toward the river" as the St. Lawrence "flexes its fingers toward the ice floes" (*Tough Romance* 33). Here, as in the Baltimore poem, water lapping at the shores of the city evoke the coming and going of immigrant populations, but also the irreversibility of the voyage. Darkness, loss, and death linger just beneath the surface of the city; the "grey arms" of Baltimore, like the flexing fingers of the St. Lawrence, grasp the metaphorical immigrant body and drag it down into darkness, as it closes its arms "round the Chesapeake, its few crabs smoldering in the deep" (*Tough Romance* 8). All that remains is the "dull glint of steel mills in the night," which has always been "the way Baltimore smiles" (*Tough Romance* 16).

The Baltimore that Di Cicco describes is that of the working class and immigrant neighbourhoods, with its "long tenements, where children play at the granite stoops" and "hospitals, that scarcely contain their blacks, their whites, their immigrants" (*Tough Romance* 16). Baltimore "weeps for no one," becoming an elusive and treacherous lover who seduces the man who "could never put his finger on the ache" until he lay silent "under a dusty mimosa in the front yard" (*Tough Romance* 16). In attempting to recuperate his father's narrative, the poet tries to experience the city through his eyes, and so he follows the elusive city "down railway tracks, behind hospitals, by steel mills, looking for her jeweled eye, and saw nothing but the glint of steel mills her one charm glistening in the bay like a mad heart" (*Tough Romance* 16). Again, here, the American city is not what it seems to be, transforming itself from glittering jewel to feminine lure that traps men through their own desire.

In the collection titled *Dead Men of the Fifties*, Di Cicco reconstructs the history of Baltimore at the height of the city's jazz age, evoking a blaring urban landscape where "each voice is so raised as to make a soundtrack for what you have shut out" (*Dead Men* 3). Vibrant scenes of music halls and jazz clubs are interspersed with the harsher realities of working-class, immigrant Baltimore with its train tracks, barber-shops and dingy pool halls. The music of Di Cicco's youth is "the carrier wave of grief, in buildings, on seashores" (*Dead Men* 3), while the public face of the city hides a threatening, lingering violence, such as "the engraving of mayhem during rioting," in a public memorial, "judges dressed like black marauders/ before a boulder-sized globe of the world" (*Dead Men* 8), and finally, the Harlem Park dwelling units which look like "stacked crates" (*Dead Men* 8) designed to more efficiently contain the city's large African-American population.

In a sweeping gesture, the narrator declares himself the poet laureate of Baltimore, his words transforming into the "public diary" of a city that too easily reveals its "broken down streets" and its "love of graves and gatherings" (*Dead Men* 11). This dark underbelly of the city is also seen in "Dirge For Sidney" where one of the denizens of Baltimore's nightlife "got it in an alley, callin' for someone's attention, a knife in the gut, the leisurely approach of two strangers" (*Dead Men* 28). The music emanating from Cora Walsh's accordion "romanced the premises," becoming a soundtrack to violence as "my pal the wolf of time snuck up on Sidney" (*Dead Men* 28) and snuffed out his life. Billy Kane, who enjoyed "steppin' to his favorite flicker house," was another "notable addition to Baltimore's slim list of murders" (*Dead Men* 28), while Johnson, the shoe-shine man at the local barber-shop who "did a job so menial as to perfect his art," falls victim to violence when he is stabbed in a street brawl.

This fascination with the illicit, with the dark corners of the city, is also found in a poem titled "The Voices Found Under the 43rd Street Viaduct, Brooklyn" where the poet ventures into the "alluring doorway" of the nightlife of the city. While the poet is attracted to New York's peep shows and shooting galleries filled with "self-inflicted victims, and suckers the size of three bands" (*Dead Men* 51), he is overwhelmed with the city's "kaleidoscope of light and clouds," and quickly realizes that he is in a "ruse-infested paradise" (*Dead Men* 51).

In *Flesh and Stone: The Body and the City in Western Civilization*, Richard Sennett uncovers how "embodiment" in the city is an historically situated phenomenon that reflects western civilization's denial of the material and social realities of the body. Taboos around the body, particularly the bodies of "others," have lead to architectural and urban practices which police the public body and assigns to each its place, function, and status. If the "master image" of the

161

body in western tradition has been male and European, such an image "inherently invites ambivalence" for, as Sennett points out, "every human body is physically idiosyncratic" (24). Thus, the bodies of racialized others or of the working poor, for instance, are marginalized – relegated to particular sites in the city and denied the same spatial freedoms that the white middle class enjoys. In his 2006 collection, *The Visible World*, we find funerals and gardens indicating two forms of escape from the city: the natural wilderness or death.

In his role as poet laureate of Toronto, Di Cicco has advocated for and celebrated urban projects which "restore the body to the city" ("2005 Remarks"), arguing that a city is understood and interpreted primarily by various forms of exchange "that are somatic, verbal and visual and yes, physical" ("Dynamics"). We see in Di Cicco's poetry a concern with how bodies have been marked as ethnically other, how they must recuperate a sense of community out of the liminal spaces of the ethnic ghetto. We also see this marginalization in his representation of the "scandalous" bodies of the homeless, trapped by a similar public discourse about what constitutes the proper and the improper. This "embodied" conception of the city is evident in his poetry as well, be it through the encounter between differently marked bodies (in terms of class, gender, or ethnicity), or through the various instances in which the city becomes an "extension" of the body of the poet. Memory functions through the body in the poet's encounter with the spaces of childhood, through his experience of the sensory stimuli of the city, and his encounters with other bodies. Furthermore, the spaces which the poet encounters also leave traces upon his body, indelibly marking his memories.

Reminiscing on his youth, the narrator walks into "the childhood of St. Zotique" where he notices a statue of Dante in the Italian quarter standing "stern in the sun" (*Tough Romance* 33). He conflates his body and the urban environment which contain his memories, as he is trapped in "the handhold of all those who are lost in their own language" (*Tough Romance* 33): "I walk towards the town, the sky on three sides of my brain, in between I am learning a new language" (*Tough Romance* 33). In "Returning to St. Dominic's," childhood friends and rivals of his years in Toronto are ghosts, spectral: "I alone exist, small ghost on a black-top, rehearsing blood-flows, the dark sky growing darker in my chest... on the corner of this street and that, the sadness begins" (*Tough Romance* 35). Here specific sites in the city evoke other spaces and moments in time, demonstrating what Boelhower has suggested of Italian-Canadian poetry, that geography is "a memory system and memory geographical" (236).

In "Travelling High," the narrator makes his way across the North American continent, "coming in from Kingston, swung round from New York state, down the flat line from Baltimore, nodding the Susquehanna into my dream" (*Tough Romance* 19). The cities of his past sit like "crowns topped on my childhood," thorny memories tearing away at the flesh of the temples. This Christian imagery of the suffering body of Christ is repeated in Di Cicco's description of Tuscany, with its "crucifixes in the shape of fathers, grandfathers, mortared steps, the bombs whistling" (*Tough Romance* 19), revealing a land and people scarred by the Second World War, but also the sense of loss which the poet feels with regards to his family history. Even a description of Venice suggests the confluence of body and space as the poet "stepped into" the city and imagined "my voice, going from street to street, like a bird among branches" (*Circular Dark* 39).

If the poet's eyes "wash over" the city from a vantage point above the fray, the city also sees him, its eyes "staring back" as it "keeps tabs on me, and me its own pulse" (*Tough Romance* 19).

This intermingling of the urban landscape and the subjectivity of the poet through the act of seeing is the same as that of the Benjaminian *flâneur*, the idle stroller who observes and records the city but attempts to remain detached from it. But, as Di Cicco reminds us, "the body has adjacencies too" (*Dead Men* 53), and these adjacencies extend to the built environments in which we dwell and the bodies with which we interact.

The workings of memory are thus described in spatial terms, in and through the body. In "Ecco," the son of immigrants who is attempting to reconstruct a narrative of displacement is "arranging footsteps backward into his life," collecting "dead things" along the way in a regression which takes him all the way back to the land of his forefathers and foremothers (*Tough Romance* 38). In "From This Apartment," the city "loses itself" in darkness as it is "claimed by naughty villains, ghostly heroines" (*Circular Dark* 26). But even in this dark, nightmarish city "love breaks open" as the narrator looks out and sees a vision of the sublime: "This geography is your genius," (*Circular Dark* 26) he proclaims, as the city stretched out before him is momentarily transformed into a frozen tableau, "a wall hanging, the sun running out of effects" (*Circular Dark* 26). The only way to escape the darkness of the city, then, is through bodily and spiritual contact, "through people, like underground tunnels, where you & I love, like escapes intersecting" (*Circular Dark* 26). The act of seeing constructs the city in a particular way, as the gaze out of doorways and windows suggests that the boundaries between inside and out, between embodied self and city, are blurred: "the skyline leers into the room, the room spills over with waiting" (*Circular Dark* 49). This "spilling over" of spatial and bodily boundaries calls into question the very notion of distinct identities, suggesting the religious, almost transcendent, experiences which the city evokes: "the landscape flowed from me, spilled over where I touched it" (*Circular Dark* 34).

Di Cicco also struggles with the allure of the city made flesh, for while the role of the poet is to articulate the transcendent by experiencing the material realities, feeling "the world looking over (his) shoulder like a conscience," he can only express "the scavenger instinct drooling its way to the poem's end" (*Circular Dark* 49). The streets elicit desire in the poet haunted by his conscience, as when he walks home alone at night "my flesh studious in itself, eyeing the streets like woman's legs, the sense of immanence gaining on me" (*Circular Dark* 49). He fears falling prey to bodily desire without the salvific power of words and poetry, and chooses instead to withdraw, "the poem falling out of my eyes & the night collected like another chance" (*Circular Dark* 49).

In "What Should a Man Do," the city is a place of "busyness, a world with madness as a prime directive" (*Circular Dark* 57). It is also a space littered with victimized bodies and corpses, both living and dead; "buses dumping bodies at subways & streets mazed like catacombs, the days of the week, carcassed beside the traffic & I am integrated, moving among people grouped like knots or pulling at each other to get free; something to fill up the years" (*Circular Dark* 57). The cacophony of the urban landscape, the rushing to and fro of people, becomes an attempt to escape the inevitability of death and mirrors T.S. Eliot's "unreal city." Bodies crammed together, pressing against one another, ironically denotes the inability to connect with others. While there may be heard "the vague emptiness of people making use of people, their lives clanking sounds of instruments" (*Tough Romance* 30), there is no escape possible, for somewhere "death grins, hungry with hosting" (*Circular Dark* 57).

In "The Oversight," Di Cicco's narrator takes a walk at night and stumbles upon a body, "drudged in the doorway, foetal, the face, folded at the toothless mouth" (*Circular Dark* 14). A homeless old man has just woken from a drunken stupor with "the dregs of his stomach" at his feet (*Circular Dark* 14). Just one week ago, the narrator remembers seeing him walk the streets, "upright, eyes fixed to the pavement... there was planning in his eyes, making room for thought" (*Circular Dark* 14). Instead, two passing boys tease and taunt him awake, evoking his anger, and the sound of protest he makes is "rooted out of him, is an extraction, is shame" (*Circular Dark* 14). In "Who Made Thee," another homeless man is "wedged against the doorway of the Nova Scotia bank," his abject body transformed into "an effigy planked in the cold" (*Circular Dark* 19). The religious imagery evoked by Di Cicco here – of the body as effigy – renders it indeterminate, uncanny – familiar to the mainstream public yet utterly "other" in its abjection. It is "spectral," as Kathleen Arnold suggests, for it is perceived as "both similar to and different from the homed... an almost-enemy (whose) presence cannot be controlled, is unpredictable, and will not go away" (78). It is a figure lying prone as if in prayer, but also a body to be reviled, cast out from the community. In its outward demeanour "sacked in a coat, straw hair leaking from his hat," it is also an "incongruous" body, threatening to the larger body

168

politic which "practices power, and creates urban form, by speaking the generic language of the body, a language which represses by exclusion" (Sennett 24).

The homeless body is therefore an "untouchable," and the boys' aggressive behaviour reveals the larger social discourse which differentiates the public body from the "errant" bodies of the homeless. They are bodies marked as abject, repugnant, and threatening to "proper" embodiment in the city. The exclusion, violence, and control directed at homeless individuals is an attempt to draw a distinct line between the proper and the improper, the homed and the unhomed. This also creates symbolic distance between the "public body" and the negative associations attached to the homeless body – alienation, poverty, filth, addiction, illness, and ultimately, death. The "war on the homeless," Samira Kawash writes, is "a mechanism for constituting and securing a public, establishing the boundaries of inclusion, and producing an abject body against which the proper, public body of the citizen can stand" (325).

While in his writings as poet laureate of Toronto, Di Cicco advocates for an urban environment based on civility, inclusion, and creativity, his poetry reveals that these qualities are often lacking; cultural loss, alienation, violence, and death are evoked in his urban landscapes. Di Cicco's involvement in Toronto's Humanitas project elucidates an engaged and informed perspective on the "creativity" of cities, which are increasingly at the crossroads of global exchanges of commerce, information, and cultural expression. Creativity is increasingly being recognized as "the central strategy to the economic and spiritual well being of citizens in a modern city," and it is primarily achieved through human encounters in the metropolis, through "curiosity, demonstration, sensation, a willingness to embrace ambiguity, balance, corporeality, connection" ("2004 Leonardo Awards"). In other words, successful cities, as Jane Jacobs demonstrated forty years earlier, are intricate, organic systems built and organized in ways that take into account the needs of individuals and communities in small scale, mixed-use neighbourhoods. Encounters in such spaces enables a "street ballet" in which residents play "distinctive parts which miraculously reinforce each other and compose an orderly whole" (Jacobs, 50).

If cities can be spaces of creativity, compassion and transcendence, they are also spaces of dereliction, violence, homelessness, and death. "The city is a poem, not a metaphor" ("2004 Leonardo Awards"), Di Cicco writes, suggesting that the modern metropolis is multiple, elusive, spectral – defying all efforts to pin it down in a single narrative. Therein lies its creative potential.

Note: Some of the talks which Di Cicco posted on the City of Toronto website were later collected in his book, *Municipal Mind: Manifestoes for the Creative City*. Toronto: Mansfield Press/ City Building Books in Association with Comedia, 2007.

Works Cited

Arnold, Kathleen R. *Homelessness, Citizenship, and Identity: The Uncanniness of Late Modernity*. New York: State University of New York Press, 2004.

Baudelaire, Charles. "Les petites vieilles." *Les Fleurs du Mal*. Paris : Le Livre de poche classique, 1999.

Beneventi, Domenic. "Heterotopias: The Imaginary Construction of Place in Italian-Canadian Writing." *Adjacencies: Minority Writing in Canada*. Eds. Lianne Moyes, Licia Canton, and Domenic Beneventi. Toronto: Guernica, 2004.

Benjamin, Walter. *Baudelaire: A Lyric Poet in the Era of High Capitalism*. New York: Verso,1983.

Boelhower, William. "Italo-Canadian Poetry and Ethnic Semiosis in the Postmodern Context." *Arrangiarsi: The Italian Immigration Experience in Canada*. Eds. R. Perin and F. Sturino. Montreal: Guernica, 1992.

Di Cicco, Pier Giorgio. *Dead Men of the Fifties*. Toronto: Mansfield Press, 2004.

——."Dynamics of Passion." Online essay at City of Toronto website, 2004.http://www.toronto.ca/culture/pdf/poet/poet_The_Dynamics_of_Passion.pdf.

——. "2005 Remarks." City of Toronto website, 2005. http://www.toronto.ca/culture/pdf/poet/2005Remarks-Valedictory_to-the-London.pdf.

——. "2004 Leonardo Awards." City of Toronto website, 2006. http://www.toronto.ca/culture/pdf/poet/2006/2004Leonardoawards.pdf.

——. *The Visible World*. Toronto: Mansfield Press, 2006.

——. *The Dark Time of Angels*. Toronto: Mansfield Press, 2003.

———. *The Tough Romance*. Montreal: Guernica, 1990.

———. *The Circular Dark*. Ottawa: Borealis Press, 1977.

Eliot, T.S. *The Annotated Waste Land*. Ed. Lawrence Rainey. New Haven. Yale University Press, 2005.

Foucault, Michel. "Of Other Spaces." *Diacritics* 16.1 (1986): 22-27.

Jacobs, Jane. *The Death and Life of Great American Cities*. New York: Random House, 1961.

Kawash, Samira. "The Homeless Body." *Public Culture* 10.2 (1998): 319-339.

Minni, C.D. & A. F. Ciampolini. Eds. *Writers in Transition: The Proceedings of the First National Conference of Italian-Canadian Writers*. Montreal: Guernica, 1990.

Pivato, Joseph. ed. *Contrasts: Comparative Essays on Italian-Canadian Writing*. Montreal: Guernica, 1985.

Sennett, Richard. *Flesh and Stone: The Body and the City in Western Civilization*. New York: W.W. Norton, 1994.

Wordsworth, William. *Preface to the Lyrical Ballads*. 1802. Ed. C. Ricks. New York: Penguin Books, 1994.

Di Cicco's Incarnational Enterprise

CLEA McDOUGALL

"I am not really there." He begins.

This pronouncement is the first thing Pier Giorgio Di Cicco says to us after a decade long pause, years of publication silence. It is this line, in the poem, "The Priest," that opens his return to poetry in *The Honeymoon Wilderness*.

With this poem he is letting us know exactly what he was up to during the silent years: becoming a Roman Catholic priest. But what does this mean to the reader? How has he changed? And if he is not really there, where is he?:

> i am not really there.
> that is what tires me. invisibility.
> it is exhausting. persona christi.
> it is not being there. leaving your body at home.
> looking forward to it.
> it is being whoever they think, the clothes they put
> on you, their love, their hate, their father;
> whoever they need; it is the ultimate acting,
> with Christ moving your lips. ("The Priest")

Di Cicco wastes no time in addressing one of the

173

central themes in his work, the paradox of corporeality – the relationship between the material and the spiritual. This conundrum, this burning question of how can we, as material beings, connect to the cosmic that was surely stirring in his early work, has special significance now. Di Cicco's self-identification has morphed into that of a priest, and the central question seems to be how does the body become a divine instrument? How can he, as poet, as priest, find a way to live with the divine in flesh, and flesh out the divine? If I have taken anything from reading Di Cicco, it is to treat my conceived dualisms as paradoxes of the highest order. The interesting thing about a paradox is that it has a possibility of resolution. Perhaps not an answer but a working out. (Di Cicco once scolded me that needing an answer falls into an Aristotelian trap. Because Aristotle says the mystery can't be known, poesis can't be thought, but it can! Not in his terms, we don't have answers for the mystery, but we can arrive at the stations of mystery, look around and recognize.)(McDougall). Dualisms stay opposed to one another. There is never an end to their polar argument. The absurdity of a paradox can in fact open up new kinds of awareness. A paradox is a work in progress:

> It was the smile before the poem, in the caress, it was the spine of ontology in everything you did, it was

174

mysterium flexing a muscle, it was grace alluding to
itself, its terminus and offspring. It was paradox lived
before duality. ("She is Not Quantifiable")

The switch in Di Cicco's self-identification is
important. If we look back to his work in *Virgin
Science,* the poetic persona is strikingly similar
to the one he presents in the opening stanza of
"The Priest":

They exhaust you on their way to God, and you like
a fool, can be anything, a liberator, a macho, a poet,
a father, a brother, a teacher, a hope. And you oblige
them. You are their means, their expiation, you fulfill all roles away from home. ("She is Not Quantifiable")

He was then, too, an object of projections, a role
player to please others. But something has
changed. He concludes the stanza from "The
Priest" by qualifying it all: "it is the ultimate
acting/ with Christ moving your lips."

In Christian theology, a priest who performs
a mass is no longer himself, he gives the
eucharist – the body and blood of Christ – "in
persona Christi," in the person of Christ. Instead
of straining on his own ego, he has let God take
over. There is a surrendering of the physical
form to God's will.

Di Cicco's poetic character has walked into
the ultimate metaphor of being a priest.

The grasping at God, the struggle with prayer that we see in his earlier work, again in *Virgin Science*...:

> I scavenge topology like a mudfish
> ready to sacralize every mote by the brute
> force of will, the dumb attraction to God,
> that is graceless ("Deep as the Exhaustion On God")

...has been let go. The self-identification in his role-playing, and the resulting frustration that exists pre-ordination, takes on a different, very physical aspect. The self has been stripped away. Remember his opening line: "I am not really there." Christ is now the actor, Christ hands him the lines, moves his lips. It is almost a state of possession. His body, he tells himself, is "a lease for Christ. And you thought you were going to the party as yourself."

He still embodies himself, through all the human worries, the doubts, the exhaustions. He says, "you could almost want to move through household furniture and have supper" and "one day you almost miss the man you were, the body at the house." But there is a sweet resignation here in place of the frustration:

> but not belonging has taken you to an abstract,
> you are perfect for it.
> when you learned to love something in everyone,
> you were done for... ("The Priest")

And though it is a shift in identification, a surrendering to God's will, Di Cicco is not promoting a denial of the body, in the classical mystic sense, in which the body is an obstacle to God, and delight in God comes at the expense of the body. This is well documented in extreme cases like Saint Catherine of Siena who would deny her body food so that she could to reach God. "Her appetite was for souls." (Flinders)

The interesting aspect of Di Cicco's stance on religiousness is that in no way is he talking about self-denial; he is not setting it up as a dualism like that. He has said: "Any humane person who knows anything about God, their enterprise has an incarnational aspect. The sane religious person knows that the divine and the earthly meet. They both have aspects of each other. They don't meet by escaping one and going to the other." (McDougall)

No, it seems, in Di Cicco's world, the affair between the human and the divine is not a dualistic proposition, as he shows us in the final metaphor of the poem, but a transformative one:

butterfly the colour of everyone's heart.
what do you want of the corpse you escaped? ("The Priest")

Works Cited

Di Cicco, Pier Giorgio. *The Honeymoon Wilderness*. Toronto: Mansfield Press, 2002.

_____. *Virgin Science*. Toronto: McClelland and Stewart, 1986

Flinders, Carol. *Enduring Grace: Living Portraits of Seven Women Mystics*. New York: Harper Collins, 1993.

McDougall, Clea. "Living in Poesis," *Ascent Magazine*, 26 (2005).

Di Cicco in the Twenty-First Century – Poet, Priest and Politico
Reflections, Prayers and Prescriptions of a Poet/Legislator

JIM ZUCCHERO

Poets are the unacknowledged legislators of the world.
Shelley

Pier Giorgio Di Cicco has led an interesting life, by any standard. Born in Italy in 1949, he moved to Canada in 1952 and spent his youth in Montreal, Toronto and Baltimore. He returned to Toronto and became deeply involved in the flourishing Canadian literary scene in the 1970s. This essay discusses two recent volumes of poetry by Di Cicco: *The Honeymoon Wilderness* (2002) and *The Dark Time of Angels* (2003). I offer a reading of these poems as personal reflection on Di Cicco's writing and thinking. My main interest is in examining how the poems "work," on both a personal and technical level. What makes them effective: first, as engaging poetry; and second, as an important contribution to the continuing development of Italian-Canadian writing? In my view, these two volumes represent some of Di Cicco's finest work. Many of the best poems are deeply personal, direct and concrete; they describe particular times, places and experiences. At the same time, they transcend these particularities, point the reader to profound existential questions, and inspire reflection on matters of personal and public importance. In probing both personal and public matters deeply and effectively in these poems, Di Cicco displays a deft touch and strikes a delicate balance. These poems reflect the culmination of his personal history and experience as an immigrant, a Catholic priest, and a public figure.

My approach is to sift through the poems looking for meaningful fragments, recurring patterns of significance, and distinctive turns of phrase in his use of language. I am especially interested in examining the relationship between these poems and public statements Di Cicco made during his term as Poet Laureate of Toronto (2004-2007). In his official role, he posted numerous monographs on a broad range of topics dealing with issues of public concern,[1] from the need for inspired, creative approaches to architecture in civic spaces, to the need for increased public courtesy and civility to foster personal and public well-being. This essay examines connections between the ideas Di Cicco expresses in these two volumes of poetry and his monographs on issues of public life. Examining the common features of this poetry and his monographs demonstrates the implicit links between the three pillars of Di Cicco's poetic disposition: his Italian roots, his Catholicity, and his dedication to cultivating greater civic generosity.

These poems explore the coalescence of three distinct but comingled aspects of Di Cicco's life – as poet, priest and public figure. At times these distinct roles seem to be integrated seamlessly; at other times a subtle tension emerges in balancing them. This tension becomes a creative energy that inspires and informs his poetic vision. We can recognize in these poems the confluence of three distinct traits: first, a strong creative impulse that has consistently found its expression in writing – some twenty volumes of poems that have spanned a thirty-year writing career. Second, there is evidence of Di Cicco's paternalism, that is, his sense of responsibility toward others which is now manifested in his ordination as a Catholic priest. In his pastoral role he is called to serve, nurture and support other sojourners; his poetry is one means of fulfilling that mission. Third, we can see evidence of his sense of civic responsibility, a duty that he feels deeply and articulates powerfully in his poetry and in his public pronouncements.

Some poems adopt the tone and even the language of some of his public speeches; conversely, some of his public comments as poet laureate have a distinctly poetic sensibility.[2] What constitutes the creative tension evident in many of these poems? How is it turned to positive effect? There is the sense that the poet is suspended (quite comfortably) in a current of temporality, between nostalgic reflection on a distant past, and longing for an elusive, idyllic future. In some poems, such as "Some Self-Reflection" and "For My Dead Mother," he reflects on his personal history and Italian cultural heritage. For example, he replays thoughts about the death of his mother and her unquestioning religious devotion, or he considers the compassion he feels in comforting his Italian parishioners in times of grief and bereavement. Other poems, like "In My Fifty-Third Year" and "The Wild Wild West," are sensual celebrations of living in the moment, close to nature. Some poems focus closely on personal acquaintances and friends (especially monks) as subjects who become catalysts for self-reflection and soul-searching. Many poems are infused with a deeply religious sensibility, characterized by a longing for a better future, one glimpsed but still distant and elusive. Much of the success of these poems derives from two key components: their conversational tone, and the careful balance Di Cicco manages to strike between dark skepticism and sunny optimism. On one hand, he offers up a clear-eyed perception of things as they are. He describes objects, individuals and social structures with a piercing awareness of their faults, shortcomings and problems. At times his descriptions are brutally honest and skeptical. On the other hand, there is very often an irrepressible sense of optimism and hopefulness apparent in these poems. Despite the recognition that life can be complicated, messy and dark, there is a buoyant sense of hopefulness about the future and a belief that things can and will be made better "in the fullness of time". This sensibility can be related directly to Di Cicco's Catholic faith, with its emphasis on the importance of genuine community and social justice. He seems to genuinely believe, and wants equally for others to share his belief, that the communities we live in, and the lives we lead, demonstrate an enormous capacity for positive growth and progress toward peace, community, and creating "the Kingdom of God."

To demonstrate the features I have described

here, I will examine some key passages in selected poems. The first section of "Marrying God" (from *The Honeymoon Wilderness*) begins as follows:

> my god blesses forks and spoons,
> and bad sex and bad livers and pontiac chrome,
> chickens and silence. he sifts crowds of busy people
> through his hands like sand and wakes me with
> new scripts. he doesn't give a hoot for health,
> he owns everything in the junk shop and says, here
> take it, walk out with it.
> my god vomits convention and spells evil like
> expectation, is soft. he has my mother's eyes
> without her edicts. his tragedy is holiness in
> special places. he blesses pots and pans in dime
> stores.
> he visits. (27)

The opening stanza of this long poem (in VI sections) sets a tone that is typical of much of Di Cicco's writing in this volume. Clearly, he is writing out of his experience of moving into a new role, as a Catholic priest. Di Cicco's God is a lower case "god"; this is an important detail. It is intended, I think, not to diminish or detract from God's status but rather to enhance it precisely by emphasizing His accessibility and His presence in the most mundane objects and events, in the very things that constitute the daily routines of life for most people, the things we tend to take for granted. The image of God "sift[ing] crowds of busy people through his hands" but also waking the poet with new scripts, is especially useful. Here, in a single line, Di Cicco juxtaposes the abstract with the personal, the monolithic with the minute. He sets out an image of the Creator who is omnipotent, holding all of humanity in His hand, and simultaneously one who knows the details of our individual lives and acts in ways that can influence us profoundly. This notion of God, which seems central to Di Cicco's personal theology, also finds clear expression in his poetry. Di Cicco invites us to re-examine the world, and our notion of God's agency in it, by suggesting that "he owns everything in the junk shop and says, here take it." The image plays on the biblical notion that the earth, in all its fullness, is God's creation, that we act as stewards for the world's natural resources. The image of the junk shop overturns the more typical characterization of the world's natural heritage as treasures to be safeguarded; similarly, the idea that it is all free for the taking contradicts the notion of ownership or privilege. (The question of how much irony he intends here is open.)

Di Cicco seems bent on creating an image of a benevolent, but also an enigmatic God, one who "vomits convention," resists the predictable, and rejects outright any notion of entitlement. Toward the end of this opening stanza his description of God turns toward the personal, with the suggestion that God "has [his] mother's eyes without her edicts." Then, as quickly, he resumes his broader scope and asserts that God's "tragedy is holiness in special places." The message implicit in his description is that attempts to circumscribe God's holiness are futile, mistaken and tragic.

In " Marrying God IV," the speaker is a first person narrator, reflecting on the day, on feelings and the lack of feelings, memories, and the tedium of daily routine; but these petty complaints are also cut by a sense of revelation, "sunlight coming through an attic window" (41). He says:

> your poetry is prayer –
> everyone joining in and
> speaking the poem with you.
> all words boil down to basics:
> love me, forgive me,
> need me, thank you. everything else
> is a warming up. (42)

Di Cicco examines the difficulties inherent in using language to try to define or describe the ineffable. Words seem wholly inadequate, yet they are all we have. In section V he writes "being married to you is not much different/ from being married to a woman, really." I assume the "you" addressed here is God. The poem can be read as his reflection, at a time when he was making the transition and adjustment from civilian life to clerical life; from life in the world of business affairs and academia, to life in a monastery or parish; from teaching, writing poetry and social commentary, to ministering to a congregation of the faithful:

maybe i don't understand the glow
of cosmicness around your baby's heart in me,
maybe the sacred shouts for dead silence,
maybe the dance is what one does before that...

There is a clear sense of confusion and mixed emotions in this passage. He expresses a human reaction to common concerns: the difficulty of balancing competing emotions and responses to the day's events. The unremarkable condition is expressed with poetic sensitivity, to stimulate the reader's reflection, meditation and perhaps even resolution.

In the lines: "the eyes of a child; they are my own, so/ gracious and so pained/ with the cross and laughter mixed" (46), the speaker's main objective is to regain a sense of wonder about the world, to approach it with curiosity, innocence and trust, or better still, with a sense of daring. The poet ruminates on the human condition, trying to make sense of experience, and his role as priest:

here i am writing madly, as prayer...
...as if a
line here or there
might expiate the botch i made of
thinking ill of others, damaging myself.
Expiation and thrill, that's me,
that's the pole i balance, walking on a highwire
while the oohs and ahhs below
both scare and goad me.
when shall i have peace? when i walk
to the other end of the wire? when i get there (47)

In this passage Di Cicco addresses writing poetry as a means of reflecting on his personal experience, his adopting a new role (his vocation to the priesthood). At the same time, he addresses much broader concerns – the human condition in general. There is an expression of naive hope ("as if...") that somehow this reflection and expression (here in the form of poetry) can be a means of atonement, or at least an exercise directed toward gaining greater self awareness about how our actions and even our thoughts toward others illustrate our true character and affect others. There is the suggestion that even thinking thoughts lacking in generosity repre-sents a debasing of our human potential. He plays on the word "pole" and examines the poles which he, and each of us, balances – the vacilla-tion between impulses of generosity and hope, or insecurity and despair – the forces that "scare and goad" us. He asks when there will be peace and offers a tentative response: when we arrive at "the other end of the wire? when [we] get there." (47) There is a nagging uncertainty and ambivalence in his response, to counter balance the notion of faith. Here he uses the poem as prayer of searching. At other points he emphasizes the poem as prayer of gratitude, of wonder, or of petition. In some poems, he sounds like the biblical Job, lamenting the plague of hardships and suffering that befall him; but, unlike Job, he is able to quickly reverse his thinking, to laugh at himself, as well as at others, as if to say: "Don't take any of this – this life, or this poetry – too seriously; afer all, it's just play, just for fun."

Exploring ambivalent feelings and responses to stimuli is a favourite tack of Di Cicco's. In the segment entitled "Christmas Suite" (which closes the long poem "Marrying God"), he describes a scene: conducting official business during the time leading up to Christmas. The poem explores the common problem of reconciling conflicting messages and impulses at Christmas time – the rampant promotion of commercialism, alongside the supposed heightened importance of spiritual matters (the celebration of the birth of Christ as saviour of the world, the mystery of God entering the world as

189

a helpless child, born in a manger, to a poor, unwed couple). The speaker conveys the sense of the practical struggle that many people experience in trying to find and preserve some genuine religious meaning and significance, amidst the crush of daily routines and social engagements which can seem overwhelming at this time of year. He addresses the baby Jesus directly: "Merry Christmas, jesus, your eyes will/ shine from some manger at some moment/ in the next few weeks/ and bring hope, you little poet you." (52) Then, he inquires about how hope works and asks: but what if we don't feel hopeful? He confesses: "I feel no shopping in me," as if shopping has become some artificially constructed measure of our commitment to the season of hope, and the deeper meaning of Christmas. There is effective use of irony here as he juxtaposes religious and commercial impulses and imperatives. Di Cicco's dark humour is evident. In another passage, he breaks down the problems of the commercialization of Christmas and examines the tensions inherent in the Christmas season for many who struggle to find some balance between social and commercial activities and the deeper religious and spiritual significance of the season. He writes:

this poem is not a present to you,
but use it, if you must...
to exchange your gift of
grace, for a memory of christmas past,
with a tag that says "what for". (54)

The notion of Christmas past is laden with meaning and can function to trigger various responses and associations. At the level of literary allusion, it can be seen as a passing reference to Charles Dickens' classic *A Christmas Carol*, a story that has become a touchstone in contemporary culture (at least in the lore of Christmas in the West, in Europe and North America). Of course, Dickens' story leans heavily on sentiment and nostalgia, emphasizing the idea that Christmases past preserve some special valuable sentiment, a precious sensibility, a simplicity and purity that has been lost. There is also the idea here that the true meaning and spirit of Christmas can be examined through storytelling. Like the Dickens tale, Di Cicco's Christmas suite can be read as an endorsement of human virtues, a narrative about hope, generosity and goodwill. At the end of this section of "Marrying God," the poet offers his poem not as a gift but as an item bartered in exchange for the gift of grace, and memory that moves us to stop and interrogate our own beliefs and actions with a simple question: "what for?"

A similar spirit of inquiry is evident in the short poem entitled "Sojourn", but it has a lighter tone. The opening lines convey the impression that the poet has been overwhelmed by an over abundance of *joie de vivre*, a spontaneous and irrepressible spirit of joy. He writes:

> sometimes I am so gosh-darned
> happy just to be writing poems not
> for someone but because the sky says
> yield what you got – (67)

What follows is a collage of images, snippets and snapshots of memory and emotion, jumbled together, out of order, linked, perhaps, by the delicate threads of emotion. He repeats the phrase "i am": "I am half-stepping in my own urine/ on the last day of my inevitable jaunt into God's/ arms; I am picking sheaves...like/ a man in me I have sent away to harvest./ ...I am happy as a boy in Montreal..." (67) Di Cicco uses the word "yield" as a recurring motif in this poem. The sky says yield; the poet yields. In the poem's closing section, he says: "it is about the door opening and guests coming/ in with flowers in their hair, each with a year/ in the hand, or several and the yield, the sky/ yields" (67). It is difficult to know how literally or figuratively to interpret the reference to time here, when Di Cicco writes "the last day of my inevitable jaunt into God's arms." The poem may have been written on the eve of his ordination, or it may simply be a reference to the emotions he was feeling at that time. (It could also be interpreted as a rumination on eschatological end time – the final judgement.) Either way, the poem conveys the poet's feeling of overwhelming well-being. In the poem's closing image, he describes a scene: "we just fill out the landscape of/ talk and moons, nowhere but in our hearts,/ so happily and in love with a planet/ riveted to our feet." (67) He gives the impression of feeling simultaneously flighty and grounded in the physical world. He captures a curious sensation, like the feeling of squishing mud between your toes – a rare sensation that can be alternately invigorating or excruciating, but one that reminds us about our close connection with the physical world we inhabit.

Di Cicco employs the simple literary device of repetition to great effect again in a striking short poem entitled "Alone". Here, the phrase "there is" is used to introduce a series of contrasting but strangely complementary images. The images are set out succinctly in progression: " there is the fear of the dark/ ...there is what can only be alleviated by/ distraction, /...there is the exhaustion of weeping./ ...there is such beauty in the leaves and trees." (91) In "Alone" Di Cicco revisits, echoes and amplifies some of the ideas and themes evident in "Sojourn" and other poems and passages in this collection. The closing stanza of the poem reads:

> there is the event of mosquito and osprey,
> of light switches and absurd history;
> any and all event, for all the good anything
> will do when they come and collect me,
> little man
> with the rage of a sunset in him
> ordinary man with a planet to spoon from.

In typical fashion here, Di Cicco juxtaposes references to the mundane and the magnificent – mosquito and osprey, things that have the capacity to be bothersome or inspiring. He makes reference to objects like light switches, things so commonplace they are taken for granted and hardly noticed; and in the next breath, "absurd history," something complex, monolithic and beyond comprehension or resolution. The final lines personalize the poem. The poet is resigned to his role as an individual in the sweep of human history and quips "for all the good anything will do when they come and collect me" (91). Still, in acknowledging his own mortality, he is not bowed; rather he asserts the absolute validity and importance of taking up the human struggle and embracing it "with the rage of a sunset." He plays on a visual image

194

from nature to suggest a connection between a natural event and his profound personal revelation; the afterglow that lights up the evening sky after the sun sinks beneath the horizon can be interpreted as a sign of the resistance to closure on the day. The final line of the poem suggests a spectacular range of possibilities for personal and collective human growth: "ordinary man with a planet to spoon from." However, it also picks up on the notion of stewardship for the physical world (evident in other poems), and the idea that we must nurture our world, since we must rely on it for our sustenance and ultimately our survival.

Structurally "Alone" is crafted into three brief segments that allow it to function as a sort of literary triptych. The first section or panel encapsulates the first stage of the poet's life and development; it contains references to youthful fears and reliance on parents. The second section can be interpreted as his movement through adulthood and toward his present condition. The third section represents his view of affairs from the third phase of his life, his present circumstance as a Catholic priest. Two other poems in this collection develop and extend the ideas touched upon in "Alone": "Cowboy on Horse in Desert" and "Imbiancato," the poem that closes the volume.

In "Cowboy on Horse in Desert," Di Cicco establishes a tone that is both conversational and somewhat whimsical. Much of the tension in the poem is created by the description of a figure caught between departure and arrival (again, reflective of the human condition). The poet identifies with the little cowboy, because he is "so lonely and never quite make[s]/ it through to the canyon arches" (98). The poet shares the cowboy's loneliness and his sense of mission; he states: "we keep each other company you and I." And yet he is also able to get beyond that sense of identification, to acknowledge a feeling of responsibility and explore his sense of steward-ship for this lonely, wandering figure. The poet's reflections on the cowboy lead him to speculate about who has created this figure: an old man, a dreamy housewife, probably not a little girl. He entertains the possibility that the figure is "a fac-tory thing" produced by some machine. The poet enters into the landscape the cowboy inhabits, and then penetrates deeper into the scene, into the cowboy's imagined conscious-ness. He surmises that the cowboy seems at peace with the lack of flowers in his environ-ment, because he "[sings] them in his heart," "[hums] under the brim of [his] hat" (99). The poet is so satisfied with the image of the cowboy he says he is "better than any Moses." He dismisses the need for any great art (including artistic depictions of Moses – perhaps a reference to Michelangelo's great sculpted marble figure). Then, in the final few lines, he admits that part of his attachment to the little cowboy is that the painted figure is static and can be clearly perceived, in contrast to the poet's inability to really see himself clearly and objectively, or to understand his own deeper motivations. He notes: "Whether I have my glasses on or not,/ I can see you clearly,/ unlike what I have made of myself." The closing lines of the poem suggest a simple truth and animate the cowboy figure one last time. Di Cicco writes: "I can wish you nothing you do not/ already have,/ and that is your wish for me" (99). The poet reflects on the cowboy, identifies with him and speculates: we want to represent our heart to others, but the world we inhabit is faulty, incorrect, full of errors and omissions. Ultimately then, we need to trust our ability to see less, and try to feel more. There is the suggestion here that progress will be made when we rely less on our capacity to perceive correctly and more on capacity to be respond compassionately to the plight of others. Although this poem is deeply personal in its subject matter and tone, the image and subject also lend themselves to being read at another level, as a gentle invocation to accept uncertainty and to act with greater generosity.

The poem that closes *The Honeymoon Wilderness* is " Imbiancato." The title may be taken from the Italian verb "imbiancare" (to whiten); the form here would be the past participle and would translate as "whitened" or "made white". It is "a note of thanks," a deep expression of gratitude. Again, Di Cicco expresses his sense of appreciation for the joy found in the commonplace objects and experiences that fill our days, and also for the mysterious things that we fail to understand. The poem has the sound of personal prayer:

Take care of me in my blindness.
Teach me to say a prayer when I am out of words.
Remind me that hope outlives the flesh.
...I admit finally, my footsteps are not my own. (115)

These lines convey Di Cicco's assertion of a profound recognition: that we control our lives only to a point and that our ultimate destiny is more complex than our capacity to exercise control over it. He offers a description of how he will embrace what life brings him:

I will walk today into the empty sojourn
of my life and look forward to the nearest stream
and that nocturnal conversation between us
where I will offer you tears

198

and you will raise them like a river between
stars and stars. (115-116)

In this powerful image, Di Cicco intimates his
belief that human suffering (the progenitor of
tears) can be transformed into something more
than what it is and can assume a more meaningful significance. Tears can become a river, a
bridge between stars. Finally, he closes the poem
with the suggestion that gratitude is the only
appropriate response to the grace we enjoy:
"There's not much more this heart would/ care
to divine./ This note of thanks I place somewhere at your feet,/ a man on the planet" (116).
The poem opens and closes on the same note:
with simple expressions of gratitude, the poet's
assertion that we are "made white," purified and
enlightened, by our recognition of being blessed,
and dedication to service toward others.

In 2002 Di Cicco published a short prose
piece entitled "The Wilderness is Yet the
Garden" – as the creative writing and social
commentary entry in *Italian Canadiana* (Vol 16.)
– in which he comments on the wilderness as a
stimulus for the composition of poetry. He
points out that the wilderness is not only physical (the natural environment); it also has psychological dimensions: the wilderness of our
consciousness and of our imagination, manifested in human interactions. He writes:

But the wilderness follows too by moths, by small signs, by every human encounter that compels us to love, even as we choose not to love; such cross-roads are the meeting place of the ineffable and us. The articulation, the mapping of such crossings are a kind of poetry that might be called "religious". But more broadly, any texture of ovation about the human existential speaks the hunger for "God," whether God is named or not. In fact, for a sublimity that avoids naming, His call to the poet is an ironic one. (113)

Di Cicco includes a poem with the same title in his next collection, *The Dark Time of Angels*. In these poems, he develops further the approach and tone he adopted in the preceding volume. Personal experience is the stimulus for reflection; in the poetry that flows from these reflective moments, he expresses his world view. The poems combine a delicate sensitivity in observance with prescriptive social commentary. They stress the need for more caring and attempt to promote the growth of a genuine spirit of human community. Examining these features demonstrates the implicit links between the three pillars of Di Cicco's poetic disposition: his Italian roots, his Catholicity, and his dedication to cultivating greater civic generosity. Furthermore, attentiveness to this focus also points out the broader significance of Di Cicco's poetry. For example, we can recognize the ways in which his poetry connects with the work of other writers of Italian origin, particularly D'Alfonso and Verdicchio who also articulate concerns about the broader social effects of writing, and the connections between writing and the creation of community. *The Honeymoon Wilderness* (2002) and *The Dark Time of Angels* take us through distinct but related phases of the poet's relationship with nature, community and the self. (Examining these volumes in relation to phases of development in the trajectory of Italian-Canadian writing can generate useful insights; they are prime examples of what I interpret as the movement into the third phase.[3])

Whereas much analysis of Di Cicco's poetics has focused on the metaphysics of his poetry, the poems in *The Dark Time of Angels* (ironically) are also important because they can be read and interpreted in ways that emphasize another dimension of his writing, one that is less abstract and more grounded in the daily, physical, temporal and communal aspects of life. Ironically, he uses angels – a most speculative and spectral subject – to reflect on the most practical, prevalent and pedestrian concerns: how we try to live together and what we can do, at practical as well as the philosophical levels, to make our co-existence better.[4]

The poems in *The Dark Time of Angels* express Di Cicco's vision, rooted in the Catholic church's teaching on social justice; it holds that the true measure of our humanity is the extent to which we care for the most vulnerable, the most needy, and those with the least power and status in society. In many of these poems, he articulates a world view that is complex: optimistic, but also critical; spiritual, but also concrete. These poems succeed, to a large extent, because he balances, and sometimes collapses the space between disparate, complex elements so skillfully – the private and the public, the religious and the secular, the orthodox and the radical. He creates short poems that can function as bridges, connecting the concrete realities of daily life with abstract concepts and theories. The end result is a poetic vision that both comforts and unsettles. It becomes a platform for personal and collective development; where individual growth and social progress go hand in hand. But the prescription is not always an easy one to embrace and follow. So, the angels are invoked as intermediaries and models; "migrants" of sorts (like the poet), who have managed the greatest migration of all, from the temporal, physical world we know, to another dimension: the eternal, ethereal world of the Creator; hence, their allure and power to inspire. Specific poems will illustrate the features I have described here.

The Dark Time of Angels opens with a poem entitled "Angel of Writing", an invocation and an excellent example of poetry as prayer, in this case a prayer of petition. The poet writes:

> angel of writing
> look after me,
> bring goodness where
> you want it, chase badness...

> heal the wounds of my forgotten.
> bring what needs to be done and undone,
> correct my every movement,
> nudge me like a blind man nudged
> gently across streets...

> do not absolve of what is not
> our business, but His.
> be thou working,
> straighten my fingers
> to the stem of wavering plants,
> give a little courage where I fear...

> my writing angels, let us not have too
> much pathos and too much laughter;
> let us keep the hearth fire burning
> just right...

> ...reshape my
> words, misbegotten by me;
> sunshine of them where my heart
> darkens, gift of evil, transform,
> leave me to burn.

be they seeds or not, my words,
rise like the morning light,
inveterately with my handfuls,
my verbiage, and let it commence,

the day for someone. (9-10)

The poem is an invocation, a clear call for guidance and a request for blessings; the poet seeks the intervention of the angel of writing (the muse?) to balance his poetic vision and assist him in composing verse that can inspire others to positive effect.

One way to approach the development of Di Cicco's poetry is to examine his orientation to the particular place he inhabits, especially, his shifting relationship with Toronto. In his preface to *Roman Candles*, the landmark anthology of poems he edited in 1978, Di Cicco said he realized, after his first return trip to Italy, that he had lived most of his life as "a man without a country." Now, more than 25 years later, his sense of the relationship between place and identity has shifted considerably. Apparently, so too has his thinking about Toronto. Now, he is a man who has found his city (if not his country) – Toronto. In numerous poems, he comments on the special quality he finds there, how people relate to each other there, how the physical space affects those interactions. He is attentive to people's sense of being in this particular urban space. From one perspective, these poems represent a marked departure from much of Di Cicco's earlier poetry; conversely, they also demonstrate a continuity and logical development from that poetry in their concern with place. Joseph Pivato has remarked that "[Di Cicco] has a profound mission to search for a sense of community among Italians in Canada and to unite them with their relatives in Italy" (251 *Lost in 3-D*). Pivato adds: "His own sense of alienation can only be alleviated if he fulfills his poetic quest" (251). I would suggest that in these two volumes Di Cicco expands the parameters of his mission; his objective now is to search for, and try to promote, a sense of community among Torontonians, Canadians, and indeed, all citizens of "the global village." His own experience – his spiritual and poetic vision – becomes his frame of reference. He searches for features of community among those who have migrated from all the distant corners of the globe, to Canada, especially to Toronto. His interest now is in those who come there to try to reconcile their diverse pasts and foster a sense of community through a shared civility that permits them to make this their new "home."

Pivato highlights important changes in the style of Di Cicco's poetry. He points out that the early poems (in *We Are the Light Turning* and *The Circular Dark*, for example) dealt more often with concrete objects and images, used shorter lines and stanzas, and simpler language. He contrasts these early poems with the form and style of later works that deal with more abstract subject matter, more sophisticated vocabulary, longer lines and stanzas. This progression is epitomized, in Pivato's view, by the poems in *Virgin Science*, a volume of poetry that moves Di Cicco "on to the intellectual mainstream of academic poetry" (255). Following the publication of *Virgin Science* in 1986, however, Di Cicco took a long hiatus and published no new collections of poems for the next 15 years. In 2002 he returned to publishing poetry with *The Honeymoon Wilderness*, and then *The Dark Time of Angels* in 2003. These two collections mark a further shift in Di Cicco's poetic style. In some ways, they seem reminiscent of his earlier more imagistic, more concrete style – the pendulum continues to swing. One reason these latest poems seem more imagistic and abstract is because they deal with more "spiritual" issues, and explore more complex ideas, than those that were the focus of his attention in his poetry in the 1970s. "Construed" (the fourth poem in *Angels*) provides a prime example of Di Cicco's later method. He takes something common and uses it as a catalyst for rumination on profound subjects; in this case, looking at the lights of a distant highway leads to reflection on the nature and meaning of God and human life. Di Cicco uses a favourite technique here, namely, the repetition of one or two motifs that resonate the larger meaning of the poem. The distant twinkling light and flies are introduced at the outset and find their way back into the poem toward the end. He begins: "from here the lights of the highway/ are distant as the purpose of the world./ God sends flies and the usual, mortgage rates..." (14). These commonplace things, the bothersome (flies) and the worrisome (mortgage rates), are juxtaposed against Di Cicco's notion of God. He suggests that God is "just a boy in summer with feet/ draped in a pool" and that he "barely hears what's/ called to him." Whereas, the need to find meaning, or make meaning in life, is a singularly human preoccupation. But Di Cicco hints that the state of childhood, with its simple focus on what is present, likely brings us closer to God than most earnest yearning. He is reminded of his monastic life, of days filled with leisurely completion of chores, but always with time to "muse about flies, as if their/ movements told the errant wisdom of God" (14). Di Cicco gently asserts that the religious quest, the desire for a deeper awareness and understanding of

God, cannot be forced or rushed. Paradoxically, it is less likely to be produced through scholarly diligence than by aimless wandering and indulgence in the physical world. Even the ardent pleas of mothers – the ever-present awareness of familial and worldly obligations – are dismissed as an obstacle to genuine communion with God. He configures these competing attractions in the image of boys playing by a pond:

> God sent them like flies, the annoying and concerned
> voices, with God giving lessons as we splashed our
> feet,
> while he spoke of grass and stars,
> of sun and bees, and the confluence felt
> like doing nothing; a placement of everything, now
> that
> I think of it, is what He taught, and the rush
> to understand was like the noise of trucks and things.
> (15)

In this simple image, and through the use of effective metaphors of flies and mothers' voices, Di Cicco captures the dilemma of trying to maintain a spiritual life, and slowing life's pace down to a rate at which we are open to revelation about the truly important things in life, in the midst of constant pressures and the hectic pace in the age of cell phones and satellites. In the closing stanza, he picks up on the opening image of lights on the distant highway and describes a feeling of awkwardness, dis-placement, and being out-of-sorts in the world: "I feel like a boy in a man's clothes I have grown into too quickly... like an orphan" with the sense "that so much meaning, as the world has, I do not miss" (15). The poet recognizes the fact that he is somehow out of step with society and the culture in which he is immersed. But he also intimates that this condition is one to be cultivated and appreciated, that it is a privilege and not a burden to him. At the same time, there is a clear awareness that living in this way is a delicate balance, one that requires time, the right climate and conditions; it cannot be forced either for himself or for others. In "Construed," Di Cicco articulates a philosophy of life, a sensibility, and a way of being in the world. He describes a state of consciousness that balances emotional and cognitive awareness, a state of being that comes as much by divine grace as by conscious effort. It is an orientation to the world that must be conditioned by a keen sensual awareness, a spirit of openness and generosity, and a willingness to accept things as they are, but also by the will to try to inspire constructive change. There are strong affinities between the world view Di Cicco articulates here and Eastern philosophical and religious precepts of the Taoist and Buddhist traditions. These concepts are explored in another of his poems, "Attendance."

In "Attendance," the poet speaks of emptiness; here, being empty, even of story, is a precondition to being open to "new music" (18). He stresses the importance of solitude and of quiet for our "brash hoping" to find fulfillment in "the kiss of cold creation" (19). The poem hints at an acknowledgment that the conditions in which most of us live make it difficult to function in this way, to tune out the noise and develop a receptiveness to the important "new music." The title of the poem begs the question: to attend to or on what? The answer implied is: the present.

"Desert Song" returns to the theme of wilderness. Although he has resisted the desert, Di Cicco recognizes the need to embrace the solitude that it represents, and the potential dangers that this solitude might conceal, to grow spiritually and emotionally. The prickly, dangerous objects and animals he names – the cactus, the horned toad, the speckled rattler, the coyote – represent the dark side of the self that must be uncovered and reconciled to move toward greater self awareness. There is a healthy willingness to face the darkness and the challenges that await him there: "it was myself/ gnashing in the dark that I needed to befriend" (22), but arriving at this point, being able to engage in these rigorous conflicts, requires a certain level of maturity that comes with age and experience. Writing poetry is part of the process; he writes: "my hungers and fears were my own, every poem/ a way to say so, slowly, ever slowly; in the twilight of/ my time, I am ready to mulch clouds and be/ my own" (22). He associates his increasing self awareness with the deepening of intimacy in his relationship with Christ. He holds Christ up as the supreme example of willingness to wander in the wilderness to gain greater humility and self awareness. The poet clearly conveys his devotion to Christ as the model human being in these lines: "I see Christ no differently than this[...] the transcendent is what you stop and gawk at/ when your fingers have brushed the/ strings of creation/ and you hear god in thistles and bramble-weeds" (22). It is striking that Di Cicco associates this transcendence not with things of sublime beauty, but rather with thorny weeds. The proposition prompts us to examine deeply our own attitudes and behaviours in seeking the divine and in our personal quest for greater self knowledge.

Di Cicco explores further the theme of pursuing self knowledge in "O Rushing Fantasy." Here, again, he engages the assistance of an angel. The poem opens with the lines: "Tonight I have swallowed my own/ by the angel's bidding" (34). The angel is the agent who leads him to confront himself: "He has brought me around to the/ place at the stream/ from which to drink either poison/ or water; depending on which day" (34). And although he finds the prospect of facing and consuming his own dark side daunting, the outcome is surprisingly positive: "I have brought myself to drink/ the foul thing that I am, and it has refreshed me/ in the dark place I had no mind to/ go to" (34). The poem revisits a favourite theme: that our selves are variably good and bad, that honest self-examination is difficult work, but equally necessary if we are to move forward and fulfill our individual potential. The scene described is reminiscent of the last judgement, a day of reckoning where "needs lie like pups on the floor" and the "ruinations of others waltz merrily past... and go out and hang themselves" calling his name. But as painful as it is, this "self-emptying" proves productive because "you see only yourself;/ and it is the beginning... you see the insufficiency, rotten nakedness" (35). The poet casts about, wondering where this exercise in self scrutiny might lead him, asking, "Oh what will it take to make me/ serviceable, this awful drinking,/ this immolation that I do myself" (35). Re-fashioning oneself requires a sort of self-annihilation. Paradoxically, the poem ends not with his sense of having arrived at some significant revelation about himself, but rather with a plea that the exercise might move him toward a greater openness to *others*: "For though I may not/ walk out of the judgement I have/ seen in myself, may others walk in and find a garden, or a leaf –" (36). The closing image crystallizes the deeper meaning of the quest for self knowledge: that it is not meant merely for personal growth, but should ultimately transcend individual change and contribute to some greater good. Here, again, Di Cicco expresses a personal theology that is deeply rooted in and measured by existence within a community.

In many of the poems in this volume, Di Cicco reflects on the nature of angels and how they function: as intermediaries, sent to act as agents for God, whose purpose is to stir and prod us toward a new consciousness. Di Cicco sets out some of his more playful theories in a somewhat tongue-in-cheek fashion in "Fighting Angels" where he cautions: "The angel must never be fought. He comes to do what he will,/ generally to smarten you up" (48). He contends that an angel's greatest impact is often achieved in its absence: "They go away, the angels./ This is how they fight you. They go away/ and leave the air blank; there is a decided lack of meaning in your life... You notice you had guidance,/ and now you don't" (48). But one gets the sense that, although Di Cicco has fanciful notions about angels, these playful ideas and images do not diminish his regard for them as a genuine force, a holy spirit that can act as a catalyst for the will of God. He notes: "They are not just porcelain and bronze,/ garden cupidons and valentines./ They are the messengers and shadows,/ they are revealers and powers" (49). The grasp of an angel is "like a choke-hold from the inside" (49). He admonishes that we must not fight the angel, although we are destined to do so, because in the end the angel's role is to help us to bend our will to God's and find out "what you are made of" (50).

"Fighting Angels" is followed by a brief poem entitled "The Wilderness Is Yet the Garden." It serves as a segue to the suite of poems that follows and sets up the progression through those poems with these lines:

> the wilderness is yet the garden
> you must see through
>
> it is the dark to be vanquished.
> it is the lone man, standing between himself
> and thistle rod.
>
> it is the dogs of chance, more terrible
> you must befriend. (51)

These are, by now, familiar images and themes:

the poet is on a quest for self knowledge, and he must be tested to gain this knowledge. The central image is one of ambivalence, conveyed neatly in the image of the garden. A garden can be a place to find nourishment, but it was also the scene of the temptation and the place where the fall from grace occurred. The garden is both a place of respite and a place of confrontation, where you may come to know yourself by the way you deal with issues and obstacles you are forced to confront, including the seductiveness of power. Effective repetition of two short phrases underscores the persistence of the encounters: "it is" and "you must" are repeated six times in close succession.

The poems that follow, under the title "Demons with Full Names," set out a series of dark visions that the poet must come to grips with before he can resurface on the other side into the light. He confronts these demons in successive brief poems with titles like: "The One Called Despair," "The Demon of Kill Yourself," "The Demon of Down," "The One Named Alone," "Panic Sprite," and finally, "The Angel That Came Through." Together these poems explore self-doubt and the tendency toward negative thoughts that must be confronted and overcome.

"Death Knocks" explores grief, despair and

darkness, and poses questions about the nature and purpose of life. Di Cicco investigates the gap not between body and mind but between body and heart, between physical presence and spiritual longing. The speaker considers the way he is, the ways in which he thinks and acts, and juxtaposes these self images against the ways he would like to behave. He concludes that "a lifetime is about teaching the heart to/ imagine" (68). He uses an effective metaphor to convey the sharp cross purposes between the body and the heart: "the body is a cousin that comes and goes,/ and the heart is a mothering thing" (69). Although we may indulge our physical life and embrace our individual physical powers periodically, our spiritual yearning is as constant as a mother's love.

In other poems, such as "Confession" and "How to Give in the World," he seems to be able to relate these two – the physical world and spiritual yearning – more readily. "Confession" strikes a deeply personal note; Di Cicco laments his failure to appreciate the beauty of the natural world that surrounds us. Reflecting on this failure, he is filled with feelings of remorse and regret. His only recourse is acknowledgement and confession; he lists his transgressions like a litany of sins: "I have failed the bushes, lilacs... I have not let birds in... I have let music be unheard... I have failed my love/ for squandering my abundance,/ the surplus of creation" (73-74). Here, the beauty of the physical world is recognized for its capacity to instill awe and wonder; the failure to appreciate this quality is regarded as not just a shortcoming but a grievous sin. In "How to Give in the World," he celebrates the physical beauty and bounty of the world in a joyful outpouring of wonder and humility: "I am paralyzed from birds and evening sun" (75).

"Changed" and "Transmogrified" extend this reflective mood but shift the focus once again, from responding to the physical world back to personal affairs. "Changed" is a reflection on the occasion of the night before his ordination. Not surprisingly, angels figure prominently; Di Cicco recounts that there were four angels with him and they brought "meaning, hope, peace, and... something that escapes me now,/ because it redeems me" (77). We might surmise that the something referred to here is grace. He speaks of being "almost transmogrified." (The term "transmogrify" is defined in the Oxford dictionary as "transform esp, in magical or surprising manner.") Di Cicco seems genuinely amazed that such wondrous changes could befall him: "blowing a kiss to the boy I was,/ half fathering him, and looking up,/ am fathered" (77). These lines suggest complex relationships:

he recognizes the continuity from his boyhood innocence to his present condition; he wants to both nurture that simplicity, and also to move beyond it to greater maturity; and he requires God's grace to achieve this emotional and spiritual growth.

In "Transmogrified," Di Cicco develops these ideas about personal change using images and objects from nature – flowers, bees, the sky and the sun – to convey his hopes. He refers to "the utter everything/ that's ours when we arraign our joy onto/ your means" and follows these lines with the image of dandelions that turn from yellow to white. The image of the dandelion is an interesting choice: the plant is ubiquitous, first as deep-rooted weed with vivid yellow flowers, then, when it matures, the garish flowers are transformed into wispy globes of seeds that scatter in the breeze to regenerate. Repeatedly, Di Cicco interjects simple, natural images into the poems to convey in graphic terms the essence of the abstract concepts, like grace and hope, he seeks to explore.

The poem that closes *The Dark Time of Angels,* entitled simply "The Prayer," is among the shortest poems in this volume. It is typical in its use of simple images from nature – snow, stones and trees – and in its method, connecting these common objects to something grand and extraordinary. The poet juxtaposes things in sharp contrast – "warm snow," stones and water, "trees lit and unlit" – and conveys the sense that he feels intimately connected with the universe and its energy. The line, "My hands unlatch the night" captures the dynamic that Di Cicco has explored throughout; the poet initiates a simple action, but in doing so he makes himself a tiny part of something magnificent. He captures this sensibility in the graphic image of the last line: "It is my breath; the stars an exhalation" (92). The poet's breath, the very essence of his being, is expelled and recognized in the stars that light the night skies.

The themes and overarching world view Di Cicco expresses in these two volumes of poetry find their parallel in many of the public statements he made during his tenure as Poet Laureate of Toronto. Di Cicco used the opportunity to launch a personal campaign to use poetry to raise people's consciousness about civic responsibility; that is, he advocated trying to heighten people's receptiveness to beauty in the physical world and promoted the idea that such a "poetic" sensitivity should translate into an increased sense of civic pride and engagement. Di Cicco has repeatedly suggested that he attributes much of his strong interest in civic affairs and his dedication to the idea of community directly to his Italian roots.[5] His political vision is simple, but profound (and consistent with his poetic disposition and Catholic mission): he asserts that we must cultivate genuine community, manifested in civility, hospitality and expressions of mutual respect for the other. These principles, which are central to Catholic teaching and ministry, would have figured prominently in the lifestyle and ethos Di Cicco experienced while living in monasteries.[6]

Di Cicco's pronouncements as Poet Laureate frequently reiterate his poetic musings, often using only slightly different language. He examines ideas about civility, public space and public art, creativity, and how we live together and try to make it work. These writings can be seen as the logical extension of his personal orientation as an Italian-Canadian, and his professional occupation as a Catholic priest. He is a strong ambassador for multiculturalism, but certainly not a zealous cheerleader for the cause who lacks critical awareness. In his postings as Poet Laureate, he offers up observations that are candid, realistic and optimistic, and analysis that is usually charitable but also incisive and sometimes distinctly edgy. The monographs are, in effect, the carefully articulated reflections and *prescriptions* of a poet/legislator. His inaugural speech as Poet Laureate, on September 29, 2004, provides clear indications of how he would approach his new role. His genuine affection for Toronto is evident; he notes that the city "has become a premiere city of diversity" and "is still a model for other cities [seeking] to enjoy the economic benefits of globalization, without surrendering their cultural humanity to the 'sameness' that globalization brings." He was quick to add that poetry should play an integral role in guiding the citizens of Toronto about how to enhance the quality of their civic interactions. He stated:

> And this is where poetry comes in. Poetry is not something sitting on a page. It is a way of life, a way of being, a way of interacting that sometimes finds its expression on the page; and the pages of poetry may teach people how to live poetically, or more precisely, with passion... Passion is about taking risks in any sector of endeavor, for the good of many and for the elevation of the human spirit. And passion is the way we encourage each other to those ends. Poetry is the record of that passion and the rallying cry for that passion.

Di Cicco often uses his monographs to explore the relationship between emotions and actions (just as he does in some poems). In a piece entitled "The Notion of Safety and Trust," he contends: "Without trust there is no risk. Without risk, there is no creativity." He sets out these concepts as if they were coordinates on a grid with an X and Y axis and proceeds to unravel the equations that work and those that break down. Trust is "a civic resource" and cities must be attentive to how this trust is eroded and eventually negated by the imposition of certain kinds of policies, bylaws and procedures. He warns that " [c]reativity will not emerge until fear has been deconstructed." With the keen insights of an artist, he points out that "creativity demands the very thing that security abhors – the unpredictable." Civility requires a certain amount of faith and sacrifice and these are indispensable as "the foundation of civility." One remarkable feature of this brief commentary is the way Di Cicco moves fluidly between dealing with issues at the macro level of geopolitics – "the world's appetite for risk is being diminished" – to examining interactions between individuals – "The 'random' is what citizens offer each other as a currency of faith." This sort of transition from the political to the personal provides a clear link between his poetry and his postings as Poet Laureate. Similarly, discussing the subject of faith is his stock in trade, and something he seems quite willing to do both in his capacity as Catholic priest, and in his role as Poet Laureate. As Poet Laureate he examines the idea of faith in a different way, not in the religious sense but rather in a secular sense, as an indispensable public virtue. He develops the idea that secular faith is akin to religious faith in that it is something that has to be cultivated – believed in and hoped for. One direct consequence of this notion of civic faith is that we create and are responsible for the world we inhabit, and for each other, personally and socially. This is an example of Di Cicco's transposing models from his religious life onto the civic arena.

Another fine example of Di Cicco's capacity to move between the political and the personal is found in his monograph "Multiculturalism and the City." Here he contends that what the "urban pilgrim wants... is identity and to find it in others by arriving at universals." He finds these universals in the most pedestrian things: "Smiles, charity and laughter are universals." Di Cicco revels in debunking what he views as false academic constructions that undermine the potential for genuine human interaction. Whereas anthropology would contend that "we need to translate cultures before we can reach each other," he asserts that in practice the inhabitants of a multicultural city like Toronto manage to create "civic decency" without any such formal translation of their cultural codes. He points out that "the blueprint of our 'getting along' has not been in our 'multiculturalism'. In the absence of a common language, we have

bridged each other through fundamentals...
[R]espect and civic decency are a literacy that didn't need programmes. A 'literacy of grace' needs no doctrine." Once again, we can find parallels between Di Cicco's poetic explorations of religious themes and his discussions of important concepts related to civic life. The literacy of grace that is required for civic harmony stems from a healthy state of mind, emotional balance, sensitivity to others, and the recognition of responsibility for our world and for each other. Di Cicco expands on this concept of a literacy of grace in various short passages in the monograph "Civic Valentines." He laments that "[c]ivic grace has been hijacked by a technology that substitutes expedience for encounter." But he is quick to describe the positive features of a literacy of grace: "A literacy of grace is based on a shared eros and joy – the eros of cohabitation on the same planet, with the knowledge of being of similar flesh, and similar thoughts and similar feelings. Diversity will mean nothing until we reclaim these commonalities." He repeatedly emphasizes ideas of the universal and concepts of humanism that stress common human characteristics and features that cut across ethnicity, gender, language, nationality and religion. He proclaims: "[e]thnicity is dead" because "ideas migrate to us before we have a chance to move."

He connects these ideas about ethnicity with popular contemporary notions about identity, conceding that post-modern individuals re-invent themselves at every turn and either associate or dismiss "the constraints of the chromosomal and the historic" to suit their particular purposes.[7] What is important to note here is that his concept of a "civic ideology," what is needed to nurture positive, constructive relations in urban settings, is compassion and it is developed by honing "the skills of care and concern." Here, again, he asserts the poet's role and the importance of language and words in promoting the sensibility he envisions: "But the eros of this mutuality cannot be strategized. It can only be inspired. And words are everything in that inspiration."

Di Cicco has used every opportunity afforded him to articulate his ideas about the crucial connection between language and human relations, and to promote his vision for revitalized civic relations. In October 2005, he gave the closing remarks at the tenth annual Metropolis conference. He suggested: "Understanding is often as simple as the language people use with each other." He examines the idea of "commonality" – what it is that binds people together, or at least permits them to be bound to one another; he concludes that it is their "core values," their wanting the same things, the mutuality of their desires, that forms the bedrock of commonality. He concedes that in the present political climate this bond can be tenuous and delicate. But Di Cicco is confident that the motivation for cooperation is strong. He suggests that "when people get along with each other it's because they have jumped to universals." He rejects the notion "that different people have different aspirations" and recommends the interrogation of that premise. He declares his faith in the idea that behind the rhetoric of multiculturalism there is a genuine universal: "behind the costumes, the politics, the agendas, the nationalities, the lifestyles, the fiscal chasms, there is a hope for the universal." In the final analysis, hope figures prominently. The mutuality of hope is the common bond that allows us to move beyond differences and toward a spirit that can inspire the genuine creativity needed to find solutions to difficult, complex problems. Finally, in the monograph entitled "Towards the Legacy of an Idea," Di Cicco challenges "city thinkers" to develop their own thinking in ways that will inspire citizens. He writes:

> ...[to] leave behind them the legacy of an idea; the statement of a simple eloquence, and the eloquent statement of an idea in a form understandable by all; for an idea that incites passion is poetry itself, and

sustains the urban dream; to leave behind the legacy of an idea at the service of passion is a great civic gift. For a citizen enlivened by passion will make an art of the city. And this notion is, at its base, hugely practical; for one knows that it is "spirit" that moves the "mind" to construct, and that "construction" without a foundation of passionate spirit is no legacy at all.

Comparing these public pronouncements with the poems in *The Honeymoon Wilderness* and *The Dark Time of Angels,* it is sometimes difficult to distinguish what sets them apart. At times we have poetry that could easily pass for social policy analysis; at other times we have social policy commentary that bears the trappings of poetry. Clearly, Di Cicco is comfortable wearing these two hats interchangeably, and even simultaneously. Through the power of his intellect and the passion of his poetic voice, he is, in the end, the best of ambassadors for the creative city he seeks to create.

In conclusion, the analysis and comments I have offered here demonstrate that Di Cicco's recent poetry, following his lengthy hiatus, represents a confluence of three elements central to his life: first, there is in his poetry clear evidence that he continues to be moved by a powerful creative impulse, one that has found its expression in poetic form for over thirty years and which has produced some twenty volumes. Second, this poetry is an expression of his "paternal" spirit. It is an artistic outpouring of the sense of responsibility he has assumed, to serve, to nurture, and to offer to his fellow sojourners his personal social analysis and prescriptions for living harmoniously, communally and creatively. Third, these poems are evidence of Di Cicco's strong, active dedication to civic responsibility. The points of intersection between his poetry and his public pronouncements suggest that the strands of these elements can hardly be separated. His public statements and his poetry share a singular quality of passion. His passion for civic responsibility, like his passion for personal religious devotion, is one that Di Cicco feels deeply and articulates powerfully and eloquently, in both his poetry and in his public pronouncements.

Notes

1. Some of these monographs have been revised and included in *Municipal Mind: Manifestos for the Creative City* (2007). At the same time that these monographs were appearing, I was engaged in an exchange of e-mail correspondence with Pier Giorgio on related topics. Our exchanges provided a lively supplement that extended the discussion of topics that he explored in his poetry and his postings as poet laureate.

2. I have never heard Di Cicco preach a sermon, but I can imagine what his Catholic homilies might sound like. I suspect that they are offered in a spirit of gratitude and humility and often lean toward invocations to greater civility. They likely draw from the same well as those poems in which he examines the ways we aspire to live together, enriched by our differences, and by our individual gifts.

3. I have suggested that the third phase of Italian-Canadian writing is characterized by two specific features: first, reference to a much wider range of subject matter and stylistic developments, more sophisticated treatment of a broader range of topics and issues (especially beyond "the immigrant experience"). Secondly, this writing is now generating a broader audience and appealing to the interests of a more diverse cross-section of readers. (See "Curried Italians" in *Strange Peregrinations* (2007)) These two collections of poetry are prime illustrations of these points. As Poet Laureate of Toronto he is a public figure whose writing touches on a wide range of topics, is circulated widely, and appeals to a broad range of readers outside of the Italian-Canadian community. At the same time, he shares an affinity with many other Italian-Canadian writers in that he assumes multiple, diverse roles at various times – as poet, critical theorist, activist and teacher. The poems in these two volumes do not deal with predominantly Italian issues or themes; rather they stem from the Italian immigrant experience but address generic, complex social and personal issues.

4. In my view, Di Cicco takes up one of the challenges that Antonio Gramsci set out in his prison writings. Gramsci championed the need for the intellectual elite to use their voices, and their positions of authority and power, to effect positive social change; to advance the cause of the oppressed and the plight of the downtrodden, and not merely to solidify and entrench their power, privilege and advantage for personal benefit.

5. An article in *Toronto Star* (B3) on October 9/04 notes: "Di Cicco went on to play a central role in an emerging generation of Italian Canadian poets. Di Cicco credits Toronto's pro-multicultural climate for nurturing his development as a citizen and as a poet." In personal email correspondence (2/24/04), Di Cicco wrote: " [I] precisely went into the priesthood because [I] saw the ethos of values at the heart of 'italianitá' had to do with a metaphysic that was transubstantive and catholic." He adds: "the 'word made flesh' was not far from what [I] was trying to do as a poet for a long time... to flesh out, to 'incarnate' the axioms of love [I] felt in the marrow of 'italianness'."

6. In 1984, Di Cicco took monastic orders at an Augustinian monastery north of Toronto. See *Globe and Mail,* October 2/04 M1-2).

7. Di Cicco has written and spoken extensively about personal and collective identity; his views on that subject merit close attention, beyond the scope of what can be accomplished in this discussion.

Works Cited

Di Cicco, Pier Giorgio. *The Honeymoon Wilderness*. Toronto: Mansfield Press, 2002.

— *The Dark Time of Angels*. Toronto: Mansfield Press, 2003.

— "The Wilderness is Yet the Garden," in *Italian Canadiana*. Toronto: U of T Press, Vol. 16 (2002), 113-117.

Pivato, Joseph. "Lost in 3-D: Di Cicco, di Michele, D'Alfonso." *The Dynamic of Cultural Exchange*. Ed. Licia Canton. Montreal: Cusmano, 2002.

Zucchero, Jim. "Curried Italians" in *Strange Peregrinations*. Eds. De Santis, Delia, Venera Fazio, Anna Foschi Ciampolini. Toronto: Frank Iacobucci Centre for Italian-Canadian Studies, 2007.

Woman and the Quest for Harmony

LICIA CANTON

I have been thinking of the long arms of peasant girls,
of cold streams where the sun washes up on the sand.
The Circular Dark, 47

Once upon a place and time, women and men
lived off the land and in harmony with nature.
The day was devoted to growing the raw mate-
rials that would be used to prepare meals. Seeds
were planted to grow the vegetables and the
wheat used to make bread at home. In such a
serene setting, five-year-old Guido spends hours
pruning tomato plants, while his mother works
the fields in the distance. (*Guido: Le roman d'un
immigrant*) Today the microwave has replaced
the wood-burning oven and it is not uncommon
to heat up something quickly and call it a meal.
Our daily combative commutes in traffic include
speeding home, getting stuck in grid locks or sar-
dined into subway cars, forced to listen to music
blaring out of the earphones of the adjacent
person. Compare that to the image of men and
women walking home at a leisurely pace across

fields, whistling and singing, birds chirping in response. Many of us associate this pastoral image to another time, another country for we come, for the most part, from a people who left small towns, hills and farms in Europe to emigrate to a North American city.

Pier Giorgio Di Cicco's poetry gives importance to ordinary people, particularly those who have an affinity to the simplicity of nature. In sharp contrast, the poet narrator raises his voice in an aggressive tone towards those who embrace the elements of the modern urban setting. In some of Di Cicco's poetry, then, the rural past is pitted against the modern present. Elements of the modern, the urban, the North American are seen as ungenuine and deserving of criticism. Images of the past, on the other hand, of things remembered in a different time and place, equated to Italy, are presented as the genuine and wholesome aspects of life. And nestled within this dichotomy is the poet's vibrant and fascinating depiction of women.

Poems such as "The Most Extraordinary Women in the World" are best read in the context of the immigrant experience and of Di Cicco's life in Toronto. Published in 1986, "The Most Extraordinary Women in the World" can be interpreted as a celebration and culmination of the many earlier poems that deal with the women in the poet's life such as "Grandmother," "My Mother Has a Photograph" and "Aunt Margaret." As Joseph Pivato writes in his essay "The Poetry of Pier Giorgio Di Cicco," these poems try to recall "the fleeting happiness of former times."

Di Cicco – the man and the poet – is best defined by his lifelong quest for harmony. His sixty-year journey is characterized by a relentless search for an equilibrium among multiple, conflicting forces: the rural and the urban, the private and the public, the material and the spiritual. He was born in the town of Arezzo in Italy set in the rolling green hills of Tuscany. By the time he was seventeen, he had already lived in two major North American cities – Montreal and Baltimore – before making Toronto his home. Thus, the rural/urban dichotomy was a major influence in the early stages of Di Cicco's life and poetry. In his thirties, he retreated from the role of public literary figure to embrace a monk's seclusion. In his fifties, as Toronto's poet laureate, his challenge was to use the spirituality of words to redirect the consumerism and materialism which drive the majority of urban residents.

Di Cicco is also defined by the possibly contradictory roles of the observer and the active participant. He is keenly aware of when "to fight" and when "to retreat." In the 1970s, as the editor of the anthology *Roman Candles*, Di Cicco brought together previously unheard solitary voices and caused a stir on the Canadian literary scene. By so doing, he united communities across Canada and gave a sense of direction to a generation of writers – and a new body of literature was born.

By the 1980s, Di Cicco had "done most things that anyone would want to do, at the age of thirty-three" (McDougall). His keen observations of people and of societal changes led to his quest for spiritual fulfillment. The modern urban environment did not meet his personal and spiritual needs. It was in his "escape" to an Augustinian monastery that he found a much yearned for spiritual cleansing from "modern muck." He withdrew from society to enter into "conversation with God" and became a priest in 1987. A life of plenty was replaced by a Spartan existence. All of these forces have resulted in very distinct focusses and poetic voices in Di Cicco's poetry: the dark, angry voice and the soothing, caring one. In his early pre-hiatus poems, the reader senses the poet's need to escape the ugliness of our world to enter the quest that would lead to spiritual harmony. The tension between these two, flesh and spirit, is evident in an early poem, "The Sundays of St. Clair" from *The Tough Romance*:

In the middle of
the night I will get up and dance on the bedsheets, out of
love for two continents.
But now I will be quiet. I am going to say the rosary of
breath so quietly. Here: the way my mother sat by my father's bed
for months in the long-windedness of his death...
(84)

Like many children of first generation immigrants, Di Cicco was raised and educated in an
atmosphere of culture clashes, conflicting mentalities and customs. In seeking progress and for-
tune, many postwar immigrants left the natural
setting of their motherland to establish a home
in the urban setting of the adopted country. A
strong connection to the old town was main-
tained through memory and a yearning for an
idyllic past. Informed by these dualities, Di
Cicco's poetry illustrates very clearly the contrast between elements of the European and the
North American.

Over the last fifty years or so, men and
women have sought and relished the benefits of
our fast-paced modern society. But at what cost?
Rereading Di Cicco's poems certainly helps to
answer this question as he juxtaposes two worlds
and two mentalities, the rural and the urban. In

"Too Much Has Resisted Us" (1977), the poet yearns for the tranquillity and simplicity of his hometown in Italy. He recalls the "June wind" filling "the cypress," his feet on "the pebbles of deserted roads," the "long arms of peasant girls." With these sensory images of the poet narrator's past, of his immigrant roots, his "heart is on fire."

Poems such as "Afternoons in May" and "The Exile," both originally published in 1977, illustrate the soothingness of spring as a substitute for Di Cicco's coveted natural setting. With the arrival of spring, "life is beginning to make more sense," says the poet narrator in "Afternoons in May." The dirty urban setting takes a backseat to the natural phase of cleansing, renewal and rebirth. As the poet marvels and praises in "Afternoons in May," "Spring is coming with both its eyes closed,/ stumbling against brick" the roads are "green with talking buds./ Huge planks of sunlight maze the roads." In "The Exile," the poet remembers a youthful time, a place he goes to via memory where "the wind just back from the cypress trees" brushes him lightly, and "in the garden the leaves are speaking of roads that empty into stillness." The images in these poems – of nature and spring, of the rural setting and uncomplicated past – are in direct contrast to the elements of the North

American city. The juxtaposition of manmade modernity and nature is rendered clearly in the personification of "spring" stumbling against "brick" in "Afternoons in May."

In his poems on families and relationships, Di Cicco often focusses on fascinating depictions of women. In the early collection *The Circular Dark,* the section entitled "Her Only Sons" deals with the poet's mother. In the striking confessional poem "My Mother Has a Photograph," Di Cicco focusses on his mother's obsessive nostalgia for a former happy period with his older brother and sister – before Pier Giorgio was born. There is a second photograph of his deceased brother in "Giorgino Buon Anima" in which the mother sees him as a kind of family martyr:

> Your blown-up photograph over
> the kitchen table
> for years (42).

On the surface, Di Cicco's representation of women recalls the Victorian dichotomy: woman is either wholesome or she is not. But in Di Cicco's poetry, setting is inevitably intertwined with the essence of woman: place is often personified as a specific type of woman. In the poem "America," for instance, there is a direct link between the "bad woman" and the filthy

North American city: she is "friendly with old drunks, with sailors" ..."a good whore – nothing to fall in love with." The new country – North America – is personified as a whore, whom no one would make his life with but would return to (in thought) every night. This depiction of the woman in the new country is in direct contrast to that presented in "Too Much Has Resisted Us," where women are "peasant girls" and "young girls in the arms of boys," exuding innocence and genuine simplicity. The poem emphasizes a sense of the natural course as wholesome and untainted. The woman to fall in love with, says the poet narrator, is not the woman-whore of the city, but the nurturing, loving woman of the idyllic setting in a pastoral town in Italy.

The contrasting images of woman and setting are clearly illustrated in "The Most Extraordinary Women in the World." At the same time, this 1986 poem from *Virgin Science* points to the socio-historical evolution of women's role, and Italian women in Canada in particular. From the perspective of an Italian-born Canadian, the poem looks at the way women used to be and the way they have become.

Traditionally, the Italian woman is the person who holds the family together – the keeper of harmony: she is the primary caregiver, self-sacrificing for the greater good of the family. This is the kind of woman that the poet narrator in "The Most Extraordinary Women in the World" would model all women after: the woman from the past, from the old country – the woman he looked up to in his youth. As Vera Golini has written, "the Italian woman confirms and affirms the character and practices that are familiar to the 'I' from the time of his innocent youth" (Golini 239). The woman presented in the first half of the poem is dedicated, above all else, to the physical and emotional well-being of children and lover:

> these are the women who hold men's faces in the palm of
> their hands, these are the women men go back to...
> They arrange for their sons and daughters the
> minute they see the sun... (11)

Complete harmony is possible – between lovers, the natural elements, children – because this type of woman adheres to maintaining the natural order. And, therefore, women like her "*are* poetry," writes Di Cicco.

In contrast, the second stanza refers to the anglo North American woman who focusses on herself: she does not firmly commit to others and, consequently, cannot maintain the natural order. That is what is fundamentally wrong with modern society, says Di Cicco: woman is not committed to maintaining harmony. She will not say "yes" readily; she uses words of uncertainty like *"would, likely, depending."* The implication is that this type of woman will discuss, argue, negotiate; she does not readily accept without questioning, reasoning or protesting. This woman is *not* poetry for Di Cicco. She has "forgotten to serve the language of lovers." She is the product of the urban North American setting and, therefore, is akin to the woman in the poem "America." The break in "The Most Extraordinary Women in the World" delineates the present from the past, the old customs and the modern ways. The poet's portrayal of women "springs in large measure from the blueprint of the Mediterranean and Latin heritage he seeks to retrieve" (Golini 239). He is disappointed and dissatisfied with "the superficial nature and the disposable character of human affections as they are lived by the North American woman in the North American ambience" (Golini 239).

To love the air is to want to fill it with lovers.

"The Most Extraordinary Women in the World" is a culturally charged poem. It speaks of emigration and immigration, and the consequences of displacing and re-rooting human beings. The poem points to the evolution of Italian women's role which has occurred as a result of immigration to the urban North American setting as well as to the socially-provoked changes in women from one generation to the next. The woman referred to in the second stanza is akin to the daughter of immigrants who no longer adheres to all the customs and codes of behaviour which her (grand)mother brought from the old country. "The Most Extraordinary Women in the World" points to the clashing cultures which have caused ruptures between mothers and daughters. The beauty of this poem is that it resonates deeply with readers – women and men – and provokes them to ponder the nature of the women who inhabited their past and those who are part of their present.

> When they dance, they dance with you,
> When they sing, it is the motherhood of half the world,
> When they go walking, they have an affair with the sunlight.

In the "The Most Extraordinary Women in the World," the poet pays homage to the women who "carried" us to the other side of the Atlantic Ocean. And by so doing, he also celebrates the motherland: Italy is the *madre patria*, the natural birth mother. What can be more natural than a mother – she who gives life and protection to her offspring? And what can be closer to harmony, than (a) mother (in) nature? This poem is an ode to a specific kind of woman: a giving, selfless person. Di Cicco's "The Most Extraordinary Women in the World" is a lament for the way a mother should to be in the natural order. This is not the modern-day mother who rushes out of the house behind schedule, drops off the kids at daycare, and does not make it home in time to feed her young. This modern-day mother *uses* English words like "depending" and "perhaps." At times, Canadian women of Italian origin are caught between the two cultures, perhaps guilt-ridden by images of mothers from yesteryear. They are searching for an equilibrium, trying to bridge the gap between the two contrasting images of woman presented in Di Cicco's poem. The depth of their cultural roots is such that some are still torn between what they have been taught – the gender roles they witnessed growing up – and what they aspire to for themselves. Many of them are hanging on to the values of their immigrant parents while aspiring to reach the goals that come with postgraduate education. Some have been successful at reconciling tradition with their modern ambitions, others not. The challenge remains in negotiating between cultures on a daily basis in order to reach an equilibrium between the modern and the traditional, the outside and the inside. Di

Cicco's "The Most Extraordinary Women in the World" focusses on the perfect woman, the Italian mother of long ago, the pre-immigration mother, the one who was not "tainted" by modern society in Canada... or in modern-day Italy.

Once upon a time, women would go to the confessional and be told to be patient, loving and tolerant... and complete harmony would reign. Once, a man had a right to treat his woman as a possession; he was expected to lead and she was expected to follow, smiling or not. This was the condition of most of the women who left the fields in Italy to work feverishly in sweatshops in Canadian cities, as well as the town seamstresses who became piece workers in the clothing industry. In the early years of immigration, as they struggled to raise their children amid strangers and unknown customs, they were still able to maintain "the natural order" within the confines of their own home. Those were extraordinary women then, as they are now, and it is their ability to retain the wholesomeness and simplicity of their youth – of another place and time – in spite of the influencing forces of modernity, which renders them extraordinary.

There may be an underlying conservative bias in Di Cicco's poem: change can be disconcerting. The reality of immigration is that it brought rapid social change in the lives of women both in Italy and in Canada. In their writing, Italian immigrant women testify that through hard work they achieved a degree of personal and economic independence which would have been difficult to realize in their native villages. There is little nostalgia among women for the restrictive living conditions of the past. We need only reread the poems of Mary di Michele, Mary Melfi and Gianna Patriarca to see the celebration of the social advancement of women. These three women, like many other Italian-Canadian writers, were able to obtain university degrees in Canada and freely achieve their career goals. Education and the pursuit of literary objectives gave these poets a voice that transcended many cultural barriers. As Patriarca reiterated in a recent interview, "for immigrant women it was twice as hard to become visible or audible, writing gave me a voice I could share with other women, especially immigrant women. It gave me a sense of visibility, strength, courage…" (Canton) Writing poetry was a source of freedom for di Michele, Melfi and Patriarca; and they gave a voice to a generation of women who lived in between cultures – the European and the North American.

In 1982 Di Cicco published "Male Rage Poem" which can be read as a stark contrast to

"The Most Extraordinary Women in the World."
With irony, sarcasm and humour he tries to exor-
cise his apparent male rage. The poet gives us a
critique of the male rage phenomenon which he
sees as having destroyed human relationships in
the modern city. "Male Rage Poem" condemns
the lack of bonding between man and woman; it
is a sharp contrast to the pastoral image presented
in the first stanza of "The Most Extraordinary
Women" where men and women do not need
words or paper to illustrate the communion
between them. In this context "The Most
Extraordinary Women in the World" can be read
as a response to feminist theory and debates on
sexual politics since Di Cicco's poem celebrates
women and their many roles in the world.

When the first wave of postwar immigrants
arrived in Canada, it took weeks if not months
to send and receive news from family back in the
small town. Today, an emailed "ciao, come stai?"
reaches relatives in seconds and the response can
be immediate. Education, mobility and technology have all contributed to changes in our
society, thereby affecting our day-to-day living.
In a few decades, we've gone from a simple,
slow-paced existence to a complicated and
chaotic society.

The force of these conflicting dualities
informs Di Cicco's poetic work. It would seem,

however, that in recent years he has reached an equilibrium between being a Catholic country priest and an international literary figure. I detected this newfound harmony in Di Cicco's voice when I called to invite him to speak in Montreal. His voice was calm and soothing on the phone. That voice belonged to Father George. It was energizing yet overwhelmingly peaceful – a stark contrast to the chaos of my modern workplace.

Works Cited

Amabili-Rivet, Rita. *Guido: Le roman d'un immigrant*. Montreal: Hurtubise, 2004

Canton, Licia. "A Conversation with Gianna Patriarca." Unpublished interview, Montreal, April 2008.

Di Cicco, Pier Giorgio, ed. *Roman Candles*. Toronto: Hounslow, 1978.

___. "Afternoons in May" in *Dancing in the House of Cards*. Toronto: Three Trees Press, 1977.

___. "America" in *The Tough Romance*. Toronto: McClelland and Stewart, 1979.

___. "The Exile," in *The Sad Facts*. Fredericton: Fiddlehead, 1977.

___. "The Most Extraordinary Women in the World" in *Virgin Science: Hunting Holistic Paradigms* (Toronto: McClelland and Stewart, 1986)

___. "Too Much Has Resisted Us" in *The Circular Dark*. Ottawa: Borealis, 1977.

Golini, Vera. "Di Cicco's Elusive Virgin: Hunting the Universal Feminine" in *The Last Effort of Dreams: Essays on the Poetry of Pier Giorgio Di Cicco*. Ed. Francesco Loriggio. Waterloo, ON: Wilfrid Laurier University Press, 2007.

McDougall, Clea. "Living in Poesis: A Day with Pier Giorgio Di Cicco." *Ascent Magazine*.

Pivato, Joseph. "The Arrival of Italian-Canadian Writing," *Canadian Ethnic Studies* 14.1 (1982). (The first published article on Italian-Canadian writers.)

___ "The Poetry of Pier Giorgio Di Cicco," http://www.athabascau.ca/writers/dicicco_essay.html

Living in Poesis/ A Day with Pier Giorgio Di Cicco

(An Interview, with My Interrupting Yet Thoughtful Interjections)

CLEA McDOUGALL

Introduction/ Suspicions of Poetry and God: Okay Let's Go

White petals are falling.
Our wineglasses slowly drain. Sarah and I talk about God, our day in Ontario, Father Di Cicco. Sarah says, There are probably lots of geniuses hiding out in the woods, doing mass.
I say, I hope so.

* * *

Before I met Father Di Cicco, I had been carrying around a napkin with his name scribbled on it for over a year. Pier Giorgio Di Cicco. That name was tucked away in my purse, in the terrible handwriting of a friend who had told me about a poet he used to know, a poet who stopped writing when he became a priest, but recently began to publish poetry again.

This interested me immediately.

Poetry and God. Two things I am slightly suspicious of, but tend to spend most of my time thinking about. It's not very often that those two things come together in an acceptable way, but I respected my friend's opinion very much, so I went to find this Di Cicco's books. When I found them, I didn't know quite what to do.

We all look for what speaks to us – poems, novels, songs – our experience reflected back, but more eloquently than we could have put it. So seldom is it that I see my own experience on the page, and not only my own present experience, but how I imagine my past and future to be.

Yet there it was.

Funny, that I find myself in a car with Sarah driving out of Toronto on our way to meet Di Cicco. I somehow knew I would meet him the moment I opened up one of his books, but as we turn off the highway, onto country roads, I wonder what exactly I am doing here.

The other day my friend who scribbled Di Cicco's name down emailed me, saying: In his most recent phase Di Cicco acts as priest – outsider as holy mediator, and as a poet – the outsider as the betrayer of brotherhood. But in doing so he also marks the very conditions of community, the finite singularity of beings divided from themselves. Put in other words, as poet/priest he is the gatekeeper to "communion."

And I thought, yes, yes... Beings divided from themselves. I am divided from myself... So, am I searching out the poet/priest to receive this communion? Maybe, maybe not, but I do feel that I will find some answers; I'm just not sure what the questions are yet.

Di Cicco lives in the Ontario countryside, north of Toronto. We get out of the car and try to find our way through the mess of country living to his door. He finds us first, squints at us through his cataracts, and after a kiss on each cheek, inquires about the colour of our eyes. He shows us around his land, gestures out to the soft hills, and says, "This is the honeymoon wilderness."

The Honeymoon Wilderness is also the title of his first book of new poetry after fifteen years. Maybe I have never spent much time with a poet, one whose work I know really well, but the day unfolds like this – at every turn are fragments of his poems, in his speech, on his wall, the dripping faucet, cactuses, the fruit-picking ladder made out of one log that reaches up to nowhere. He leans against it and I say, you wrote a poem about that ladder. It's the first time all day that I call him on it, and he looks at me with a particular expression of mistrust and astonishment; maybe he was surprised that I actually read his poems, I don't know.

The land is wild and untended. His house is spare and accented with 1950s furniture, some kitschy Catholic nick-knacks, a few books (ranging from vintage fiction digests to Derrida for Beginners), old records, and not much else. On the wall is a painting of Route 66, complete with blinking red lights. He's a mix of backwoods hermit, high-talking philosopher, man of God and Canadian poet. He gives weekly mass, teaches at the university and has recently been made the poet laureate of Toronto. His priest's collar lies on the kitchen table alongside ashtrays and coffee cups. This is where we spend most of the day.

We Begin/What the F*** is Metaphysics?: A Lesson

But at first we sit in his living room. I'm glad Sarah has come along, because she is occupying Di Cicco with grandiose arguments of dualism. For the time being, I get to sit back and observe. Very quickly I know what we are in for. Poet

Dennis Lee has described Di Cicco as "gregarious, intelligent, cantankerous, lonely, droll, obsessive, impulsively tender." And I would have to agree with him.

Di Cicco begins like this, and it is typical of how the day follows:

I hate to jump on the old bandwagon, but the bad guys still appear to be the Greek philosophers. But what is it that presupposes a people to become dualistic? We tend to look for psychological, philosophical, social, anthropological answers to this, and this is very easy for us to do, because we are a very non-somatic society. We don't think in terms of the body in North America or Nordic countries, and the answers may be in the intelligence of the body and not in the body of the intelligence.

The metaphysics of any people are predicated by land and the environment that they are from. What is it in ecology that predicates thinking, feeling and reasoning? As central a thing as light. As light. The light in the Mediterranean is very dramatic. It goes from sky to earth. There's a movement you can see and feel, a movement; it's like the light of heaven shining on the Earth. You've got two things already that predispose you against a metaphysic of one joining with the other.

***

Sarah leaves to load the camera and poke around the grounds. I try getting background material on Di Cicco's life, but he acts bored, and isn't having any of it. I can't tell if he is avoiding answering my questions, or just doesn't like the subject matter. He wants to engage, and he doesn't want me to be the interviewer. At one point our conversation goes like this:

How has being Italian affected your poetry?

What do you mean? Why do you ask that?

I don't know, it was your segue. You started talking about poetry, then said how Italian you are. Are they connected?

I'm still trying to figure that out. It would look like the attempt to reconcile oppositions like Italian and American, Med and North American would seek to find its resolution through the arts, but I don't think so.

I've realized lately that we tend to explain much of what we do by socio-cultural-anthropological backgrounds. But in fact, we are propelled by a metaphysic. And that metaphysic gives birth to the cultural, not vice versa. Culture has become God in the twentieth and twenty-first century. We think everything is explained by culture. I don't believe that to be the case. As I was mentioning earlier, just as the light predicated philosophy, metaphysics predicates the culture.

The way Italians make an arc of a gesture with their hand, that's simply a gestural mimetic of the relationship between what is around the body and the body. Our bodily expressions are expressions of our relationship to the land. Our thoughts, our syntax, are predications of that, our cultural habits are predicated by that. So that my poetry was a result of a certain kind of metaphysic...

Let me take a rest. Let me think. It's not wise to think rapidly. When you think rapidly, you are forced to syntax, to narratives, to scripts that may not be genuine. That's why the poet takes time writing. So as not to fall into predictable and handed scripts. I trust myself in poems; I don't trust myself in conversation.

That's interesting, because you like conversation.

Yeah, I especially like it because it can become a poem. That's the best part of conversation. Mostly it doesn't; mostly it's dialogic. And poetry is not dialogic.

What is it?

The poem is always about becoming one. The poem creates oneness in itself and draws the reader into oneness. It seeks to become. It seeks to become the reader. The dialogic doesn't seek to become, the dialogic likes separateness. It's a difference between the unitive and the binaristic. My metaphysic has always been impelled to the unitive. I suggest that all metaphysics, all people are impelled to the unitive, but by apparently different strategies.

And your strategy has been poetry and prayer.

Yes, poetry and prayer... I need a glass of orange juice. Do you want more Pepsi?

No, I still have some.

A Bit of Background/Why He Became a Priest: Making Eggs

I do manage to squeeze a few biographical details out of him. Pier Giorgio Di Cicco was born in Arezzo, Toscana, Italy, in 1949. His family moved to Montreal when he was three, but he grew up mostly in Baltimore and considers himself of the particular Italian American breed. He moved back to Canada in the late 1960s to attend the University of Toronto and live among the thriving Italian-speaking community.

He published his first book of poetry in 1975, *We Are the Light Turning,* and went on to publish over a dozen books until he moved to a monastery in 1983. After four years he decided to become a priest and for the last seven years has been "a country priest, which in some way duplicates the best aspect of hermitage."

Di Cicco's exit from the literary community in the 1980s was abrupt and unexpected. "Art" and "Religion" are two institutions that, when entered into at a very serious level, are often exclusive of one another. The boundaries are not usually transcended, and yet Di Cicco has made this movement seem fluid and effortless. And it also seems as if he just doesn't give a shit what people think. He prays, he writes. "What difference does it make if you write on paper or on your heart?" he asks me.

Maybe we could talk about the time in your life when you decided to become a monk. I'm curious about the time leading up to that, how you made that decision and what impelled you toward that life.

Well, I had done most things that anyone would want to do, at the age of thirty-three.

Yes, but what attracted you to prayer?

I had gone through an intellectual conversion. I had just finished a book called *Virgin Science,* which was a poetic restructuring of holistic paradigms that were available, and psychology and physics, quantum mechanics, holographic theories of consciousness, you name it. Back in the 1980s when these things were beginning to be popularized; now they are sort of household ideas. I thought I would take that route, looking for a scientific apologia for spirituality... but... Why don't you turn that off and let me have a couple of eggs. I'm a little peckish.

***

I lean against the kitchen counter, trying to look at ease, a false grace I affect when I am nervous but want to seem as if I know what I am doing. The act of turning off the recorder loosens him up and breaks apart the awkward relationship of interviewer and interviewee.

What I really want to know from him is how and why he became a priest. I want to know for this article, but also as a person who has had thoughts of "religious vocation." I want to know what it takes, what happens in a life, so that the decision can be made, the step taken.

But how did you start to pray, why did you go to the monastery, what was your life like then, the circumstance that made this happen, how did you make the decision? This is something I need to know. You were my age then...

And between the melting butter, the empty eggshells, he tells me. He was my age then.

***

I sneak the recorder back on. The sound of eggs frying.

And were you bored with yourself?

Yeah! I need to be excited, I needed an intellectual conversation, I needed to be inspired. I needed to be... fulminated, epiphanied. Looking back on it now, who else but God could excite? Who else understood physics and poetry, or whatever, the most esoteric; who else was I going to go to? The Internet? Like everyone is doing now?

That's why prayer came in. Prayer. You see, I

could talk to God about anything and he would listen. I needed to hear him. I didn't hear God for a long time because I was mentalizing him. You know how I did that? By not talking to him. Vocal prayer is essential. If we are body, and you can't leap from the somatic condition in prayer, then you have to pray through the body; that means talking to God the way I am talking to you now. Excuse me! (*he shouts at me*) I'm talking to you... I'm not thinking about you. I mean you're real, body, voice, touch. Hello... People say, Oh, well, God is an abstraction. Well, he's an abstraction if you treat him like an abstraction... God speaks through the self-revelations of the somatic, kinesthetic. And the body is kinesthetic, because when you talk with the body, the mind and heart come together. When kinesthesis is reached, then God's presence is manifest. Hence people feel the presence of God at parties – why? Because they are somatic with the incarnational components of each other. The rest of the time they go home.

In yoga, the holy trinity is body-mind-speech...

Yes, exactly. The phonocentric is essential in prayer. People come to ask me how to pray. I say, have you tried just kneeling in your apartment and looking up and talking to God, you know what I mean? We don't want to look ridiculous to ourselves, do we? And sometimes that's all it takes. You're going to feel ridiculous to yourself if you say to someone you haven't known for long, but you feel like you're in love with (*grabs my arm*), I think I love you. Because you don't know! You might get slapped back, rejected. Well, God is no different than a lover. You know? He loves you but, I'm sorry, he wants you to come out and say, I think I'm in love with you! These are such basic things!

We are called to talk, to unite. We are called to recognize and be recognized. We are called to recognize the indistinguishable, the inextinguishable, the appetite, hunger – that's the metaphysic. We are all called to the unitive, but some are called with particular passion. It sounds elitist, but some are called with particular passion. As near as I can tell, there simply are more passionate people and less passionate people. It doesn't mean that the less passionate people aren't all walking toward the unitive. But some have to run.

Broken Hearts/ *Living in Poesis:* We Have Coffee

It is near the end of the afternoon. We are all sitting at the kitchen table. The way he talks about

259

a unitive metaphysic sounds to me like the idea we have in yoga of liberation or enlightenment, or moving (maybe running) toward something we think could be freedom. So I ask him:

How do you understand liberation?

We have this idea that we want to be free. *[Laughter.]* We don't understand that being free means saying goodbye to things that we are not ready to part with yet and don't want to part with and some things that we will never be ready to part with. You know, there is this gung-ho wholesale run toward the embrace of total freedom. The price of that is ominous; the cost of that is ominous. Not in terms of what we pleasantly call risks. The freeing of yourself may involve the loss of yourself. That's a nice idea, because we have this idea of self as this ego, as this barking little dog, that once we get rid of it, the house will be tidy again. But I mean self, who you are, recognizable to yourself by any demonstrable means. That's a scarier proposition. Not just throwing out the dog, but the furniture as well.

You know the dark night of the soul is more than just a psychological overhaul. A lot of us think it is. I want to be free on my own terms; I want to be holy on my own terms. Being holy, I don't know much about it, but it seems to me that it's about having your heart broken so many times that you don't have a heart anymore. You don't have a heart anymore.

Well, you have heart, but it's a useless paradigm, 'cause hearts are meant to be mended. What if they're meant to be broken and have water run through them like the Colorado River through the Grand Canyon? I mean, everyone wants a heart that can be mended. But what if we are not called to a mended heart? Scary. I for one am not ready to surrender the metaphor of a heart that can be mended. I'm fifty-four years old; I'm still not ready.

Let me make you some coffee. Turn that thing off.

***

Sarah and I sit in silence for a while, contemplating the possibility of a heart that is not meant to be mended. Di Cicco conducts the day with these odd and stunning metaphors. It is at once exciting and exhausting. I think, *where am I?* Here we are, at a very regular Formica kitchen table, in a rather empty kitchen, at an ordinary house in the country. But he keeps saying things like... this is as palpable as the flesh, as the style of love and the texture of someone's benevolence.

What do you think of that? It sounds rather...
poetic.

Poetic, eh? I did three public lectures at the university this year, slamming Aristotle. I had everyone believing that they were in poesis. As soon as the lecture was over they slipped back down the slippery slope of dualization, of thinking that thinking and feeling were two different things. The whole point of being a good metaphysician is that you can have a thinking feeling and feeling thought. That's the binarism to stitch back together right there. If you can do that, you can do anything.

It's not as if intelligence is outside the heart; it's not as if mind is without feeling. But how do we manage to be that way? Language goes a long way to defeating us. What perpetuates the dualism, is language. It perpetuates linear thinking. That's why poetry is good for non-linear thinking. Syntax is within Newtonian time, past, present and future. Poetry, which I claim is where we mainly live, whether we admit it or not, is in the timeless.

Have some cream.

Sadness/ We Arrive at the End of our Day: Sarah Takes a Picture

It's starting to make sense to me now. I described reading his poetry at the beginning, as being able to imagine my own past, present and future. But that perhaps is an overly ordinary way of describing it. There is something irresistibly touching about his poems, that tugs on the reader, tugs one out of the regular sequences of time. Maybe that is what all poetry does. Maybe that is what prayer does, too. Di Cicco is someone who sincerely practises both, and in that practice, his voice takes on a certain transparency that lets you walk right in.

The day is ending. I ask:

Has your life changed by becoming a priest? Where is this path taking you?

I'm not on any path. I'm just going back to what I was, the origins. Everything's a journey these days. When you think about things in terms of journeys too much, you lose sight of the fact that you may have arrived. It's so popular to say journey journey journey, and so unpopular to say arrive arrive arrive, that even if you've arrived, you're afraid to say so or even admit it to yourself. Every poem is an arrival. I can say it's part of many poems, which are an ongoing journey. Well, what's the point of that?

My point is not to have an overview of many points of arrival; my point is to be lost in arrivals as they happen, because the back doors – each one has a trap door that leads into the timeless. Not back into narratives of Newtonian time. Journeys are about narrative, narrative is about Newtonian time, the timeless is what we want what we are where we live for the most part. Where we are from. It's not where we are going, the timeless is not where we are going; timeless is what we flip into at any given time, when you stop the mental strategies of narrative.

***

The phone rings. Di Cicco has to get ready to give mass, at his church in the city. Sarah is fiddling with a piece of plastic on the table, and I say, *Sarah, that's his priest collar*. We laugh and wait for him to get off the phone.

I don't know if I can ask him this next question or not. It's been on my mind all day. *Are you sad?* It's a simple enough question. And I don't know whether or not to tell him I have spent hours reading his poems and crying. Literally, tears run down my face. It sounds a little crazy.

I haven't quite figured out what the crying is all about.

Anyway, all I can force out is:

This just might be me... but I find a lot of your poetry quite sad. So, uh, are you sad?

Am I sad? *[long pause.]* The sadness, is, uh... is the frustration. Some people are very appetitive, and are always asking that the bar be raised before it is raised. I'm always asking that the bar be raised before it is raised. And the sadness comes out of that. Sadness is the result of not knowing what we want to know, when we want to know it. I am very appetitive about the rendering present of God, and God rendering the Divine present. And when I am frustrated by it, I get impatient. I can rest, but I am also restless. So the sadness comes out of restlessness. Wanting things that I am not supposed to want.

From God or from the world?

From God, I'd say. What does the world have to offer? Not much, as far as I can tell. Maybe other God searchers like you...

Click.

Sarah explains:

There's more light coming in, that's all.

Research Notes on the Poetry of Pier Giorgio Di Cicco

Joseph Pivato

This collection of essays on Pier Giorgio Di Cicco is not the final word on this fine poet. Each essay is meant to stimulate further reading and thought on his literary works and on Canadian literature. In these brief notes I try to articulate some possible directions for further work on Di Cicco's poems. Some readers may have other suggestions.

The poetry of Di Cicco can be read in the context of the immigrant experience in Canada and in the context of national and international literary influences. Before the acceptance of post-colonial theories in North America, these two approaches, the biographical and the intertextual, were considered incompatible by academics and literary scholars. In my own long academic training in Comparative Literature and theory, we learned the axiom that "Works of literature are the products of other works of literature, and not necessarily a reflection of the life experiences of the author." And we were discouraged from using biographical or sociological information in our interpretation of literary works. My work in ethnic minority writing caused me to question all of these assumptions derived from formalism and the New Criticism.

Reading Di Cicco, I soon realized that the ideals of an impersonal are not only false, but probably bad art as well. The serious study of ethnic minority writing teaches us that writing is personal and political. And these observations are supported by post-colonial theories and feminist theories. Ethnic minority writing is concerned with telling the stories of displaced people, with examining questions of identity and with giving voice to those who have been silenced. The biographical element is at the centre of this writing. In the course of composing and publishing his many poems Di Cicco has told these forgotten stories and given voice to lost and silenced people.

A close reading of Di Cicco's poetry also reveals the literary influences of a wide circle of Canadian and international authors. So within this poetry we find both the personal and the intertextual. I will briefly explore some of the echoes of other writers in the works of Di Cicco. What we find is that a parallel between a poem of Di Cicco and that of another writer makes us reread both works in new and different ways. A clear example of this is the literary parallel and contrast between Di Cicco's poem, "A Man Called Beppino" and Mary di Michele's poem, "How to Kill Your Father." We read Di Cicco's homage to his dead father in these moving lines:

> The man who lost his barbershop during the war
> loves great white roses at the back of the house beside
> a highway. The roses dream with him,
> of being understood in clear English, or of a large
> Italian sun, or of walking forever on a
> Sunday afternoon. (1979, 11)

A comparison also brings out contrasts in the treatment of ideas, points of view, irony, voice and images. In di Michele we find these lines of conflict with her father:

> You are alone on the highway to the sun
> Your north American education
> has taught you how to kill your father,
> but you are walking down an Italian
> way, so you will surrender
> and visit him in the hospital
> where you will be accused
> of wishing his death
> in wanting a life
> for yourself. (1980, 36)

It does not matter which poem was written first, or which poem was the first influence, because each poem affects the reading of the other poem and in the mind of the reader they will be linked for a long time. Such links suggests that it would be fruitful to do a detailed comparative study of these two poets.

In addition to the work of di Michele, the poems of Di Cicco could be compared and contrasted to those of Pasquale Verdicchio in *This Nothing's Place* (2008), and Gianna Patriarca in *Italian Women and Other Tragedies* (1994). There are about fifty Italian-Canadian poets writing in English, in French or in Italian. And there is the potential to consider several other comparisons.

In his 1985 essay, "Contemporary Influences on the Poetry of Mary di Michele," Robert Billings identifies the circle of literary friends and acquaintances which di Michele and Di Cicco shared in Toronto during the 1970s and 1980s. He first lists four women poets as important influences: Roo Borson, Susan Clickman, Bronwen Wallace and Carolyn Smart. The larger group includes Barry Dempster, Kim Maltman, Albert F. Moritz, David Donell, Tom Wayman and Joe Rosenblatt. Many of these authors continued to publish poetry into the 1990s. What would a comparative study reveal about the echoes among these writers?

There are a number of other Canadian

writers who come to mind in comparisons to Di Cicco's work. In interviews, Di Cicco speaks fondly of the poems of Al Purdy and Irving Layton. He particularly admired Dennis Lee's *Civil elegies and other poems* (1972). (Pivato)

Among American poets Di Cicco often refers to the work of the deep image poets like James Wright and W.S. Merwin. Robert Bly's translation of Latin American poets: Pablo Neruda and Cesar Vallejo promoted neo-surrealism. In Bly's poetic meditations, we are reminded of Di Cicco's elegiac moments in *The Dark Time of Angels* (2003) and *The Visible World* (2006). In the literary background of all these poets are the work and ideas of the imagists who focus on the clarity of the language, exactness of detail, concrete references, and shorter poems. The best known are Ezra Pound and Amy Lowell.

In addition to Neruda and Vallejo, the other name which appears in Di Cicco's collections is the Spanish surrealist poet Federico Garcia Lorca. His social criticism of urban society found in *Poet in New York* (1940) is echoed in such Di Cicco poems as "America," and "Remembering Baltimore, Arezzo." Lorca's striking images are in every poem:

Debajo de las multiplicationes
hay una gota de sangue de pato. (98)

Di Cicco speaks, reads and writes in Italian. In several of his collections of poems he quotes from Italian writers: Dante, Salvatore Quasimodo, and Romano Guardini. Are there Italian influences in the poems of Di Cicco? In Quasimodo's *Giorno dopo giorno* (1947), we find a humanity and hope that reminds us of Di Cicco's socially conscious poems. We see this in Quasimodo's "Lamento per il sud":

> E questa sera carica d'inverno
> è ancora nostra, e qui ripeto e te
> il mio assurdo contrappunto
> di dolcezza e di furori,
> un lamendo d'amore senza amore. (265)

Edoardo Cacciatore's preoccupation with science and language, with the question of mind and body in his poetry collection, *Graduali* (1986), reminds us of Di Cicco's *Virgin Science*. The meditative elements in Andrea Zanzotto's *Elegia e altri versi* (1954) seem to be echoed in some of Di Cicco's poems. We see this in Zanzotto's "Ecloga IV":

> "Dolce" fiato che muovi
> le nascite dal guscio, il coma, il muto:
> "dolce" bruma che covi
> il ritorno del patto convenuto. (430)

In Italian there is an expression about the immigrant experience, "Parte anche chi rimane." It tries to capture the loss to Italy of the departing immigrants by focusing on the disruption to individual families. "Even those who remain behind leave." This is captured by Janni Sabucco in "Elegia dell'Ontario," writing about his immigrant father who went to Canada:

Quest'Ontario amato da tuo padre
non lo potrai mai esorcizzare. (17)

Works Cited

Billings, Robert. "Contemporary Influences on the Poetry of Mary di Michele," in *Contrasts: Comparative Essays on Italian-Canadian Writing*. Ed. J. Pivato, Montreal: Guernica, 1985.

Bly, Robert. Ed. and Trans. *Neruda and Vallejo: Selected Poems*. New edition, 1993.

Di Cicco, Pier Giorgio. *The Tough Romance*. Toronto: McClelland & Stewart, 1979.

Di Michele, Mary. *Bread and Chocolate*. Ottawa: Oberon Press, 1980.

Lorca, Federico Garcia. *Poet in New York*. New York: Grove Press, 1955. Bilingual edition.

Pivato, Joseph. "The Lost Interview with Pier Giorgio Di Cicco," (1985) posted online 2008 on Athabasca University Canadian Writers site under Di Cicco.

Quasimodo, Salvatore. "Lamento per il Sud," in *Twentieth-Century Italian Poetry*. Ed. L.R. Lind. New York: Bobbs-Merrill, 1974.

Sabucco, Janni. *Geografia d'Occasione*. Padova: Bino Rebellato, 1967.

Zanzotto, Andrea. "Ecloga IV," in *Twentieth-Century Italian Poetry: An Anthology*. Eds . Picchione & L.R. Smith. Toronto: University of Toronto Press, 1993.

Brief Biography
of Pier Giorgio Di Cicco

JOSEPH PIVATO

Arezzo is a town south of Florence in the Region of Toscana in central Italy. This is were Pier Giorgio Di Cicco was born in 1949 in a landscape still ravaged by the Second World War. He had an older sister born in 1930 and an older brother who had died from a bomb blast in 1944. In 1952 his family emigrated to Montreal, and then to Toronto in 1956. They settled in Baltimore in 1958 where his father later died. In 1967 he and his mother moved to Toronto to live with his older sister. He attended the University of Toronto were he earned a B.A. in English (1973) and a B.Ed. (1976). Growing up in an immigrant household was difficult and Di Cicco tried to reject his Italian heritage until his first trip back to the country of his birth in 1974. This trip was an epiphany which awakened his Italian identity and began his quest for a space in the English Canadian literary landscape. These events in his early life are often reflected in his poetry. We should also note that Di Cicco speaks fluent, standard Italian which is the language of the Toscana region, and this too is evident in the vocabulary of his poetry.

While in university Di Cicco had begun to write poetry and to publish in student magazines. In 1976 his poems were included in Al Purdy's *Storm Warning II*. His first book of poems, *We Are the Light Turning*, appeared in 1975 and in a revised edition in 1976. He was now living in downtown Toronto and working as an editor with *Books in Canada*, later with *Waves*, *Descant* and *Poetry Toronto*. He was also participating in many poetry readings in competition with other young poets who had migrated to Toronto's lively arts scene. He read at John Robert Colombo's Harbourfront series.

Colombo's Hounslow Press later published *Roman Candles*, an anthology of Italian-Canadian poets edited by Di Cicco in 1978, which marked the beginning of the phenomenon of Italian-Canadian writing.

In the meantime Di Cicco had published a succession of books in rapid fashion: *The Sad Facts*, *The Circular Dark*, *Dancing in a House of Cards*, *A Burning Patience*, and *Dolce-Amaro*. In 1979 his first important collection appeared, *The Tough Romance*, and marked the positive influence of Chilean poet, Pablo Neruda. This volume was translated into French as *Les*

Amours difficiles (1990). In his books *Flying Deeper Into the Century* (1982) and *Post-Sixties Nocturne* (1985), he continued to demonstrate the influence of Italian and Latin American writers. His style of deep images also includes a strong dimension of philosophical abstraction in *Virgin Science: Hunting Holistic Paradigms* (1986) which was the last book he published before he committed himself to the religious life in a monastery north of Toronto.

In September 1986 Italian-Canadian writers from across Canada gathered in Vancouver for a conference on the issues of ethnic minority writing. During that conference they decided to establish the Association of Italian-Canadian Writers. In addition to Di Cicco the founders included Antonio D'Alfonso, Pasquale Verdicchio, Antonino Mazza, Mary di Michele, Marco Micone, Dorè Michelut and myself. Some of these writers were aware of the fact Di Cicco had entered a monastery in about 1984 but did not know that he would leave the life of the professional writer. In the meantime the Association of Italian-Canadian Writers thrived and held conferences every two years in a different city.

Di Cicco stopped writing and publishing for fifteen years. During this time he left the monastery and began training for the priesthood. He earned a Master of Divinity degree in

1990 and was ordained in 1993. He worked as a parish priest in four large churches using his Italian language skills and in a small country church north of Toronto.

In 1999 he began to write once more and *Living in Paradise: New and Selected Poems* appeared in 2001. Then came *The Honeymoon Wilderness* (2002), followed by *The Dark Side of Angels* (2003). In 2004 Di Cicco was made Poet Laureate of Toronto, succeeding Dennis Lee. Later he was invited to be visiting professor in the Italian Studies Department at the University of Toronto. The books continued to appear: *Dead Men of the Fifties* (2004), and *The Visible World* (2006).

During his tenure as Poet Laureate, Di Cicco worked to promote creativity in all aspects of city life from city hall and city planning to life on the street. He collected his series of talks in a book, *Municipal Mind* (2007).

Selected Bibliography of Pier Giorgio Di Cicco

Books by Pier Giorgio Di Cicco

We Are the Light Turning. Toronto: Missing Link Press, 1975.

We Are the Light Turning. (revised ed.) Birmingham, Ala.: Thunder City Press, 1976.

The Sad Facts. Fredericton: Fiddlehead Poetry Books, 1977.

The Circular Dark. Ottawa: Borealis Press, 1977.

Dancing in a House of Cards. Toronto: Three Trees Press, 1977.

Editor. *Roman Candles: An Anthology by Seventeen Italo-Canadian Poets.* Toronto: Hounslow Press, 1878.

A Burning Patience. Ottawa: Borealis Press, 1978.

Dolce-Amaro. Alabama: Papavero Press, 1979, (limited edition).

The Tough Romance. Toronto: McClelland and Stewart, 1979. Reprinted in Montreal: Guernica Editions, 1990.

A Straw Hat for Everything. Birmingham, Ala.: Angelstone Press, 1981.

Flying Deeper Into the Century. Toronto: McClelland and Stewart, 1982.

Dark to Light: Reasons for Humanness. Vancouver: Intermedia, 1983.

Women We Never See Again. Ottawa: Borealis Press, 1984.

Post-Sixties Nocturne. Fredericton: Fiddlehead/ Goose Lane, 1985.

Virgin Science. Toronto: McClelland and Stewart, 1986.

Les Amours difficiles. Trans. Frank Caucci. Montreal: Guernica Editions, 1990. (*The Tough Romance* in French).

Living in Paradise: New and Selected Poems (Afterword by Dennis Lee), Toronto: Mansfield Press, 2001.

The Honeymoon Wilderness. Toronto: Mansfield Press, 2002.

The Dark Time of Angels. Toronto: Mansfield Press, 2004.

Dead Men of the Fifties. Toronto: Mansfield Press, 2004.

The Visible World. Toronto: Mansfield Press, 2006.

Municipal Mind: Manifestos for the Creative City. Toronto: Mansfield Press and Comedia, U.K., 2007. Talks by Di Cicco as Poet Laureate of Toronto.

Poetry included in Anthologies

Purdy, Al. ed. *Storm Warning II*. Toronto: McClelland and Stewart, 1976.

Gist, K.P. ed. *This Is My* Best. Toronto: Coach House Press, 1976.

Gatenby, Greg. ed. *Whale Sound*. Vancouver: J.J. Douglas, 1978.

Colombo, John Robert. ed. *The Poets of Canada*. Edmonton: Hurtig Publishing, 1978.

Dempster, Barry. ed. *Tributaries: An Anthology*. Oakville: Mosaic/Valley Editions, 1980.

Ricker, Marvi. ed. *Sharing Through Poetry: A Multicultural Experience*. Toronto: University of Toronto, 1980.

Wayman, Tom. ed. *Going for Coffee*. Vancouver: Harbour Publishing, 1981.

Atwood, Margaret. ed. *The Oxford Book of Canadian Verse*. Toronto: Oxford U.P. 1982.

Di Giovanni, Caroline M. ed. *Italian-Canadian Voices*. Oakville: Mosaic Press, 1984.

Norris, Ken. ed. *Twenty Canadian Poets of the Eighties*. Toronto: Anansi Press, 1984.

Lee, Dennis. ed. *The New Canadian Poets*. Toronto: McClelland and Stewart. 1986.

Alfonsi, Ferdinando. ed. *Poeti Italo-Americani*. Catanzaro: Antonio Carello, 1985.

Kamboureli, Smaro. ed. *Making a Difference: Canadian Multicultural Literature*. Toronto: Oxford U. P., 1996.

Loriggio, Francesco. ed. *L'Altra storia: Antologia della letteratura Italo-Canadese*. Vibo Valentia: Monteleone, 1998.

Pivato, Joseph. ed. *The Anthology of Italian-Canadian Writing*. Toronto: Guernica Editions, 1998.

Lee, John. ed. *Body Language*. Windsor, On.: Black Moss Press, 2003.

Di Giovanni, Caroline M. ed. *Italian Canadian Voices: A Literary Anthology 1946-2004*.

Oakville: Mosaic Press, 2006.

Books on Pier Giorgio Di Cicco

Loriggio, Francesco. ed. *The Last Effort of Dreams: Essays on the Poetry of Pier Giorgio Di Cicco*. Waterloo: Wilfrid Laurier University Press, 2007.

Articles, Interviews and Essays

Lorenzini, Amleto. "Intervista a Pier Giorgio Di Cicco," *Argomenti Canadesi*. Rome, 1978.

De Iuliis, Celestino. "Interview with Pier Giorgio Di Cicco," *Quaderni Canadesi*. 3 (1978).

Interview, *Corriere Canadese*, Toronto, July 5, 1979.

Loriggio, Francesco. Review of *Roman Candles. Quaderni d'italianistica*. I, 2 (1980).

Di Cicco, "Ethnicity and Identity," Panel with Maria Campbell, Andrew Suknaski and Rudy Wiebe, in *Identifications: Ethnicity and the Writer in Canada*. ed. Jars Balan. Edmonton: University of Alberta, 1982.

Pivato, Joseph. "The Arrival of Italian-Canadian Writing," *Canadian Ethnic Studies*. XIV, 1 (1982).

Pivato, Joseph. "The Return Journey in Italian-Canadian Literature," *Canadian Literature* 106 (Fall, 1985).

Amprimoz, Alexandre & Sante A. Viselli. "Death Between Two Cultures: Italian-Canadian Poetry," in *Contrasts: Comparative Essays on Italian-Canadian Writing*. ed. Joseph Pivato. Montreal: Guernica Editions, 1985.

Pivato, Joseph. "Documenting Italian-Canadian Writing," *Italian Canadiana*. I, 1 (1985).

Padolsky, Enoch. "The Place of Italian-Canadian Writing," *Journal of Canadian Studies*. 21, 4 (Winter, 1986-87).

Billings, Robert. "Interview with Pier Giorgio Di Cicco," *Poetry Canada Review*. 18, 1 (Fall, 1986).

St. Pierre, Paul Matthew. "Pier Giorgio Di Cicco." *Dictionary of Literary Biography*. ed. W.H. New. Vol. 60. Detroit: Gale Co. 1987.

Iannucci, Susan. "Contemporary Italo-Canadian Literature," in *Arrangiarsi: The Italian Immigration Experience in Canada*. eds. R. Perin & F. Sturino. Montreal: Guernica Editions, 1989.

Boelhower, William. "Italo-Canadian Poetry and Ethnic Semiosis in the Postmodern Context," in *Arrangiarsi*, op. cit.

De Klerck, Denis. "Protean Apologist of Love." *Cross Canada Writers' Magazine* 2.2 (1989).

Di Cicco, Pier Giorgio. "Perspectives," and "Notes Towards a Poetic Manifesto," in *Writers in Transition: The Proceedings of the First National Conference of Italian-Canadian Writers*. eds. C. Nino Minni & Anna Foschi Ciampolini. Montreal: Guernica Editions, 1990.

Pivato, Joseph. "Italian-Canadian Writing: A Polysystem," in *Literatures of Lesser Diffusion*. eds. J. Pivato, Steven Totosy & M. Dimic. Edmonton: University of Alberta, 1990.

Pivato, Joseph. "Oral Roots of Italian-Canadian Writing," in *Echo: Essays on Other Literatures*. J. Pivato. Toronto: Guernica Editions, 1994

Blodgett, E.D. "Towards an Ethnic Style," *Canadian Review of Comparative Literature*. 22, 3-4 (1995).

Pivato, Joseph. "Challenging the National Literature: Italian-Canadian Writers and Others." *Palimpsesti Culturali: Gli apporti delle emigrazioni alla letteratura del Canada*. ed. Anna Pia De Luca et al. Udine: Forum, 1998.

Pivato, Joseph. "Lost in 3-D: Di Cicco, di Michele, D'Alfonso." *The Dynamics of Cultural Exchange*. ed. Licia Canton. Montreal: Cusmano, 2002.

Loriggio, Francesco. "Pier Giorgio Di Cicco at the Turn of the Century: Interview." *Italian Canadiana* 17 (2003).

Pivato, Joseph. "The Early Poetry of Pier Giorgio Di Cicco." *Italian Canadiana* 17 (2003).

Senyshyn, Yaroslav. "The Hegelian Exhaustibility of Art and Dante's End of Philosophy: Existential Thought and Polymetric Music in Di Cicco's Poetry." *Italian Canadiana* 18 (2004).

Pivato, Joseph. "Twenty Years of Change: The Paradox of AICW," in *Strange Perigrinations: Italian-Canadian Literary Landscapes*. Eds Delia De Santis, Venera Fazio, Anna Foschi Ciampolini. Toronto: The Frank Iacobucci Centre for Italian-Canadian Studies. 2007.

Pivato, Joseph. "The Lost Interview with Pier Giorgio Di Cicco," (1985) posted online 2008, Athabasca University Canadian Writers site under Di Cicco.

Acknowledgements

I would like to acknowledge the following people:
Pier Giorgio Di Cicco for the dream about an Italian-Canadian Literature.

Antonio D'Alfonso for conceiving this Writers Series and publishing Canadian authors for over thirty-three years.

Mary di Michele for supporting this book project.

George Elliott Clarke for writing that Italian-Canadian writers are a model for other ethnic minority authors and groups.

All the contributors for their cooperation and patience.

The Association of Italian-Canadian Writers for continuing to promote writers.

Athabasca University for giving me leave time to work on this book project.

And my wife, Emma Pivato, for her assistance.

*

Stacey Gibson, "Seeking the Divine," was first published in the *U of T Magazine* (Summer 2005).

Mary di Michele, "Living Inside the Poem," shorter version in *The Last Effort of Dreams*, ed. Francesco Loriggio (Wilfrid Laurier University Press 2007).

Linda Hutcheon, "Canadian Ethnic Ironies and Di Cicco's Poetry," edited excerpts from *Spitting Images: Contemporary Canadian Ironies*. Toronto: Oxford U.P., 1991.

George Elliott Clarke, "Let Us Compare Anthologies: Harmonizing the Founding African-Canadian and

Italian-Canadian Literary Collections," *Belonging in Canada: Immigration and the Politics of Race and Ethnicity. Proceedings from the19th Annual Reddin Symposium*. Ed. Mark Kasoff. Bowling Green, OH: Canadian Studies Centre, Bowling Green State University, 2006. 37-57.

Clea McDougall, "Living in Poesis," was first published in *Ascent Magazine*, issue 26 (2005).

Cover photo of Pier Giorgio Di Cicco is by Kevin Kelly Photography (Toronto).

Contributors

Domenic Beneventi was SSHRC post-doctoral fellow at the Université de Sherbrooke (Québec) where he teaches. His research project focusses on the representation of homelessness in Canadian literature. He is co-editor of *Adjacencies: Minority Writing in Canada* (Guernica, 2003), and has published articles on minority and urban literatures in Canada.

Licia Canton has a Ph.D. in Canadian literature for the Université de Montréal. She has edited *The Dynamics of Cultural Exchange* (Cusmano 2002) and co-edited *Writing Beyond History* (Cusmano 2006) and other books. She is editor of *Accenti Magazine*. Her collection of stories *Almond Wine and Fertility* (Longbridge) appeared in 2008.

George Elliott Clarke is a poet, novelist, critic and librettist. He is the E.J. Pratt Professor in Canadian Literature at the University of Toronto. His publications include: *Whylah Falls* (1990), *George & Rue* (HarperCollins 2005), *Black* (Polestar 2006) and *Odysseys Home: Mapping African-Canadian Literature* (U. of T. Press 2002). He turned his play *Beatrice Chancy* (1999) into an opera which was performed across Canada.

Mary di Michele is a poet, novelist and professor at Concordia University in Montreal. She was one of the original seventenn poets in *Roman Candles* (1978). Her last book of poems is *Debriefing the Rose* (Anansi 1998). Her novel, *Tenor of Love* (2005) has been published in Canada, the US and appeared in Italian as *Canto d'amore* (2006).

Stacey Gibson is a writer who has served as Managing Editor of the *U of T Magazine* at the University of Toronto. She has written on literary and historical topics.

Linda Hutcheon is Canada's pre-eminent literary critic who has published several significant books among which are: *The Politics of Postmodernism* (1989), *Irony's Edge* (1994), with Michael Hutcheon, *Opera: Desire, Disease, Death* (1996). *A Theory of Adaptation* appeared in 2006. She taught Comparative Literature and English at the University of Toronto until her early retirement in 2009.

283

Joshua Lovelace earned an MA from Simon Fraser University (Vancouver) with a thesis on poet Roy Kiyooka. He did an MFA at Bard College, New York.

Clea McDougall is a Toronto writer and Editor of *Ascent Magazine* in Toronto. She has written on the arts, literature, and life-style issues.

Joseph Pivato (Ph.D. University of Alberta) has published a number of books on Italian-Canadian writing including *Contrasts* (1985, 1991), *Echo* (1994, 2003), and edited *The Anthology of Italian-Canadian Writing* (Guernica 1998). He teaches literature at Athabasca University in Edmonton.

Jim Zucchero earned a Ph.D. in English with a thesis on immigration history, memory, ethnic identity and Italian-Canadian writing. He is an academic counsellor at King's University College, University of Western Ontario. Jim has published essays on Nino Ricci, Mario Duliani, Maria Ardizzi and Penny Petrone.

Printed in March 2011
by Gauvin Press,
Gatineau, Québec